Virtuous Woman Remix

Virtuous Woman Remix

For Powerful Queens and the Kings Who Benefit

Michele A. Bryant-Roberts

Copyright © 2020 by Michele A. Bryant-Roberts.

ISBN:	Softcover	978-1-6641-2143-0
	eBook	978-1-6641-2142-3

All rights reserved. No part of this book may be reproduced or transmitted in any form or by any means, electronic or mechanical, including photocopying, recording, or by any information storage and retrieval system, without permission in writing from the copyright owner.

The views expressed in this work are solely those of the author and do not necessarily reflect the views of the publisher, and the publisher hereby disclaims any responsibility for them.

Scripture quotations marked KJV are from the Holy Bible, King James Version (Authorized Version). First published in 1611. Quoted from the KJV Classic Reference Bible, Copyright © 1983 by The Zondervan Corporation.

Scriptures marked as "(CEV)" are taken from the Contemporary English Version Copyright © 1995 by American Bible Society. Used by permission.

Scripture quotations marked NIV are taken from the Holy Bible, New International Version®. NIV®. Copyright © 1973, 1978, 1984 by International Bible Society. Used by permission of Zondervan. All rights reserved. [Biblica]

Any people depicted in stock imagery provided by Getty Images are models, and such images are being used for illustrative purposes only. Certain stock imagery © Getty Images.

Print information available on the last page.

Rev. date: 08/05/2020

To order additional copies of this book, contact:
Xlibris
844-714-8691
www.Xlibris.com
Orders@Xlibris.com

Contents

Introduction vii

Chapter 1 Creation: Tell Me What Happened 1
Chapter 2 They Fall and Could Not Get Up 4
Chapter 3 How to Maneuver around the Consequences of Sin and Win 13
Chapter 4 Her Seed Has Come 23
Chapter 5 What Is She Really Created to Do? 29
Chapter 6 Add It Up 50
Chapter 7 No Clue 54
Chapter 8 Preacher on a Sunday Night 62
Chapter 9 Who Is This Jezebel Anyway? 64
Chapter 10 Being Virtuous Will Happen 68
Chapter 11 Here is How You Win 73
Chapter 12 Started in Fear and Wins in Power 74

Afterthought 81

Introduction

I am not going to discuss what happens all over the world, but I can say that I have read a few things and have heard more than enough stories. In the United States, women did not get the right to vote until August 18, 1920. That was called women's suffrage. This only happened after hundreds of years of activists working to prove that women deserved the same rights as men because they are just as much citizens of this country as men are. What is really going on? There has been a struggle for equal pay in sports and the workplace and even how men handle their wives at home. If you are reading this in another country, I am sure that you will be able to reconcile much of the same sentiment.

When I started to write this book, I researched the fact that women's movements sprang up all over the world at various times. Where did all of this start? Let me first be honest with you: I am not very educated in the plight of women's issues. It was around 2007 when I was way grown and my children were way gone. My pastor's wife asked me to head up a women's class with a subject of my choosing. I was at a loss. I was desperate and put out the word to a few of my close female associates. One of them gave me a book about women in the Bible. That was the first time that I read the book of Ruth in the Bible. Yes, I am a woman, but I have never really related to movements. But yet, here I want you to subscribe to this movement that started in me back in 2009. That was the year I published my first book, and it was about whom women were created to be. This book is more extensive than that one. All of my research at that time was scriptural references and how they impressed personally on me.

This renewed interest has included some information that was previously "hidden" from me about how women are really situated to function on this earth. I was probably ill-equipped to receive what the initial research was trying to tell me.

I grew up under the guidance of a preacher for a father and a dedicated preacher's wife for a mother. I rebelled. I did not want to live like them. It was probably because they wanted it more for me than I wanted it for myself. I ran away from God (Daddy and Mommy) and joined the army. After three years of that, I was still not ready to go with God. I ran to college (not a bad choice). After that, there was nowhere else to turn where I would feel safe. At least the army gave me a cot, meals, and uniforms; college tuition included a dorm room and three meals a day. Now I was a veteran and a college graduate with no real direction. Besides that, I had gained a son and a husband along the way. While my husband remained in the military stationed overseas, I tucked my tail with my son in tow and went back to my home state of New York. Not home a month and my life changed; I surrendered to a new set of orders. I turned my life over to God. My mother and father were overjoyed. God had won!

It would be another thirty-plus years before I came to realize that I was a woman, and there was a world around me that struggled in that arena. I was surviving marriage now living in Georgia. Surviving is what I had always learned to do without the crutch of being a victim of any circumstance. What I had heard as a child from scripture about women was reinvigorated in me during the study for that 2007 class. I became excited about the information, especially watching many women around me mess up with their men, not know who they were as women, and blame all of their woes on their relationships. The information that I found had to be taught. In 2009 I went to work. The book, *The Woman's Curse and You*, was a study on how women could overcome the consequences of the curse pronounced on them after the original sin found in the book of Genesis. It was at this time that I believed I had an answer to what ailed many women. It ailed me too, but I had never related to any of my personal issues as being universal with women. I had always believed that my struggles were personal and just things I had to learn to overcome.

Finding solutions has always been my forte. When trouble comes, what is the answer? In 2007 I realized that many women were not as fortunate as I was with the early teaching that came from scripture. They squirmed under the pressure of demanding men and those men that would not bend under the pressure of needy women. Then there are the men who do not know scripture either and make life difficult for women who live with them as they follow rules that are manmade old traditional values. There are the women who think men were created just to please them and others who want to "mother" and control men. There is an answer, but you have to be willing to open up your mind to new thoughts. Solutions are the result of working through the difficulties until the true answers appear. They are usually inside of you and must be awakened.

My marriage turns forty on October 15, 2020. Being a virtuous woman has always been one of my goals. Many people say that Proverbs 31 could not be talking about one woman with all of the many duties she handled. I beg to differ. It is really not that hard. This is not just a statement of debate. Read the rest of this book and see what this means. In forty years I have been many things and done many things and am still handling many things. This book is only the discovery of information that has always been here. I still have more to discover!

You must decide to study how women and men can coexist while fulfilling their God-given purpose on this earth. That is a lifetime class. There is always something new to learn and obstacles to overcome. It is really not difficult. It may require some mind adjustment to reestablish what was always supposed to be, which got twisted along the way. If you are one who lives in an always perfect atmosphere with your other, you can stop reading now. If you can see a need for some improvement and are willing to hear some other perspectives, keep reading. God had a plan and is still willing to manifest it to those who are willing to listen and apply.

One of the largest concerns I have heard from women is *when* they make adjustments to how they function in different relationships how this will affect their love relationships. Now if you are single and unattached, this will run smoothly. Make all the changes that you need because the next love interest you connect to will meet a new and improved you. If you are already in a committed relationship, you will also be fine. Men are waiting for that next phase. The change you make will not be for them, but for you. How do I know this will work? Because I did it, and watched my marriage turn 180 degrees. It takes a strong man to embrace the power intrinsic in virtuous women. It takes the wisdom of powerful women to know how to interject assets in a relationship and they not become disruptions to peace. If done right, all modifications *will* be welcome.

The Bible has a plethora of information on this topic. The one theme that stands out is the stories that make up the peace in the war called the battle of the sexes. This journey to some discovery has taken me eleven years. Writing on the subject did not take up all those years, but reconciling with scripture the old truths I had subscribed to was a job within itself.

The desire for this writing is that it presents a clear illustration of the reason you chose to read *this* book. Women are a powerful entity. Just because many are still crying for equality does not diminish their place in society, whether it is acknowledged by all or not. Pay her more, let her vote, let her run for office, etc., etc. When all of this is done, is a man feeling any different toward women, or are women feeling vindicated for what has happened over the years? In my *opinion*: "No!" It's just as foggy as a war on racism that calls for all hearts to be changed, embracing the fact that all men are equal. That is not the job of a human. I want open hearts to this writing so that those who want to think differently about a woman's role in society can embrace what the foundation of that looks like.

Knowing why women were created is a good place to start. You must first believe that there was a real thought process in creation. If you want to know why something was created and how it works, you go to the creator of that thing. This may not work for you if you believe in a big bang that had no definable thought from a thinking describable entity. But if you subscribe to a semblance of creativity, this book will make complete sense.

Misunderstanding and ignorance have been at the forefront of most negative interactions between the sexes. Who are you and why are you here? Answer that question and you will have greater success as the great woman you are created to be. Think of it this way, no matter where you find yourself, who you are can shine through giving you victory even if the people around you do not change. A young man is homeless. He wins a contest that lasts for a week, giving him a chauffeur and a limousine to take him to a five-star restaurant every day. The young man stands at his corner every day waiting for his ride. He enjoys his daily outing, but never decides to upgrade his lifestyle. Is the limo driver any less of a driver because the young man did not change? Who you are is why you are great. The homeless man was disciplined enough to meet every day for his ride and you (the limo driver) had enough passion to do your God-given purpose. Everyone is satisfied. Never misunderstand your purpose and do not believe for a second that it is your job to judge and change those around you. Work on being the best you can be, and things will systematically change around you, even in your relationship(s).

If the homeless man above was asking for advice, I would tell him what he could do to change, but for now, I'm answering those who are constantly asking and in pursuit of better love relationships. You are at the top of your game because you are asking for and willing to change. If you are great, you can even be greater. Get the principles that can change your life. God has some advice for you.

Men, I hope that you are reading this too. It was never meant for you to bear the burden of doing life alone. You can be alone but not lonely, or you can have a woman that knows who she is and will be good for you. Women were created to be a helper to you. Okay, that may sound archaic, but if you keep reading, you will begin to understand the dynamics of the male/female relationship. Each sex living out its purpose is a blessing to both sexes. The press in me to write this is for both men and women to be enlightened.

This book is not so much about connecting in marriage as it is about embracing what you were created to do. You could already be privy to this information, but I can guarantee that most of you will hear something new or have a different perspective of some previously known information. Knowing the purpose of a thing makes its operations valuable to you. Learning how to use all the functions makes you wealthier. That goes for cars and humans.

Take your time and inhale the essence of how you read. The best directive is to read what is written here as if you have never heard any of it before. The more you learn, the more you realize how little you really know. Breathe and read.

When you are done, I believe what you will sense is refreshing. During the reception of some of the information, you may have to denounce what you once thought you knew. It is not disrespectful to your heritage, but a reformation of some old information. You want to know the truth that will make your walk in this life more enlightening about the God who is in control. The information is just as good as when you had your first crush. Remember that feeling?

The word "remix" is in the title of this book because the story of the virtuous woman is not new. The nuances of the twenty-first century have brought a new and rewarding light to an old story. The rhythm is still the same, but there are a few added verses. These verses jumped off the pages of the Bible during this study. When some producers remix songs, they maintain the integrity of the tune while often changing syncopation and sometimes adding lyrics. This is the picture of this book. The virtuous woman has been remixed and updated for the twenty-first century.

For all you Bible scholars, those who believe that life will never be perfect until there is a new earth, you are right. God just made a way for his people to escape the curse and the consequences of it just by renewing their mind. The perfection of the Garden of Eden will never again exist on *this* earth, but God fixed it so that you can still win with his perfectly designed tools. Keep reading and it will all come clear. The perfection on this earth will be in your perfect perception of what God always wanted for those He loves.

I have heard the word "virtuous woman" all thirty-plus years that I have committed my life to being a believer. I do not believe I have ever understood it the way I understand it now. I will not say that no one had the capacity to help me to understand, I just may not have been ready to receive it.

Let me remix it for you. Women should still strive to be virtuous (morally excellent/right standing with God). This is not to say that you do not make mistakes; it is to say that your heart is to do the will of God. There is no greater attribute than to live a life consistently aligned with what you were created to do. Add the understanding of living in God's Kingdom here on earth and you get as close to perfection as is humanly possible in a world with temptation all around. Remixing, simply put, is updating.

Men, you get the benefit of a woman who wants to help you in the areas that make you great. Now you are the king with a beautiful queen on your side. There is nothing more gracious than women who know who they are and men that can do nothing but appreciate the gift. Appreciation is reciprocal. "Who can find a virtuous woman? For her price is far above rubies (Prov. 31:10)." What man does not want that? And, what woman does not want to be described as being worth more than rubies? A woman that knows her worth and a man that appreciates it is a match intended by God.

Running for public office or homeschooling four children, let's remix how a woman can choose her own place based on desires, make a man happy he found her, and be someone to be admired, all while adding value to wherever she finds herself. This was all planned from the beginning; let's remix it and hear it again for the first time.

Note: You may see the word "submit" as it pertains to women submitting to their own husband, but don't take it as subservient. It is only a matter of order. Walking in his purpose, the man too has a part to play in the comfort of his wife (1 Cor. 7:4).

Chapter One

Creation: Tell Me What Happened

This is the story of how the man and the woman got together; the story gets skewed, a remedy is created and then continues with peace as a permanent pursuit. It is a psychological thriller, so you must pay attention to each detail. It has always been meant for the man and woman to enjoy each other's company, but of course, there had to be a spoiler. The story continues today as the man and woman continue to seek to capture what once was. The peace was lost, but still exists to be found.

God does his work in heaven and shares responsibility for the earth with humans. This takes faith in what God has promised mankind. There is only a small segment of society that has absolutely no faith. God gave everyone the measure, but some just choose not to use their portion. Large segments of the population still believe that creation is a real concept. Well, this is the story of creation and the continuation of it. All creation has a beginning and evolves into what it is supposed to be. An acorn is what starts a towering oak tree. But before that, it began in the mind of God. Everything begins in heaven and spreads out across the physical universe. God is the creator of it all and knows how to orchestrate an end to the bad that man brought on himself. (Except where indicated, "man" refers to both man and woman.) You only need to follow the route that leads from heaven to where you live. You can see how everything genuinely fits together when you follow God as He directs the plans.

When the Earth was created, it was only a big ball with nothing in or on it. All of a sudden appears land, seas, and then most animals that would eventually be known to man. All of this creation took God five days. Now exists on earth, land, water, and animals. Earth, at this point, is designed with the ability to sustain life.

It was on day six of creation that God's greatest work for earth would manifest. Out of the ground came all the remaining animals. They joined the beautiful vegetation that God had delayed up in heaven before He had created someone to take care of it (Gen. 2:4–5). Now that the animals are here along with vegetation, man will be made to run it all.

Out of the soil of the earth, in God's likeness, God forms man. This powerful being has the ability to reason and make decisions. God is a spirit, but in his sovereign power made man spiritual in a physical shell. He is to rule the earth under God's guidance.

Man named all of the animals according to what he saw. He had the responsibility of taking care of the earth and dominating all of its other inhabitants. Genesis 1:26 said, "And God said, Let us make man in our image, after our likeness: and let them have dominion over the fish of the sea, and over the fowl of the air, and over the cattle, and over all the earth, and over every creeping thing that creepeth upon the earth." All the animals had mates and with that attribute came the ability to procreate.

Man ruled the earth. He was given only one commandment with negative consequences for disobeying. In this magnificent land stood all the food for the man to gather and satisfy his appetite. The tree of life even had its place with its ability to keep man alive forever. But there was also the tree of the knowledge of good and evil. Eating from it would cause death. God warned man not to eat of this *one* tree. (In a moment, the reason for this will be explained.) With all of this greatness, there was something wrong. After all this was done, God noted that man did not have any help. Man being alone was not a good thing. God loved man, and man loved God, but man had no one to physically demonstrate his love to and no one to carry his seed. Procreation was necessary to fill the earth. The word "replenish," in the early words of Genesis, means to fill and complete. It would be man's responsibility to do this. God saw man's aloneness and decided that in order to fill his assignment, he needed a helper.

"And the Lord God said, It is not good that the man should be alone; I will make him a help meet for him" (Gen. 2:18). Although the word "man" in the Bible represents the human species, the male was created first and then God decides to give him a wife. No human should be alone, but history has shown us the balance of the male-female relationship. The balance is that women are excellent, at their best, in the supporting/partnership role alongside men. Of course, when it comes to things in the spiritual sense, there is a blurring of roles. When all come together in Christ, there is no male or female or separation of cultures (Gal. 3:28). God had a big plan. He would get man a mate right out of the man's own body. What better mate can you find than one that is created out of the same stuff as itself? The first-ever surgery was performed by God, and it was done on the first man. Man was put under to get his eventual partner out of him. God removed a rib. Ribs, in the human body, have three important functions: protection, support, and respiration. This one rib God removed would be the foundation of what would eventually become a woman. When the woman was formed and Adam awoke, he immediately called her woman because she was taken out of him. She would later receive a proper name. This is somewhat funny because Adam, the man, never did get another name! Both Adam and the woman were referred to as Adam (Gen. 5:2). The name Adam refers to the Hebrew word for man or another word meaning red because of the color of the original human's skin tone (Behindthename.com). Here is something to think about, why didn't Adam ever get a proper name? Hmm! God could have created another man identical to the male Adam, but that would have defeated the purpose of procreation (you know that part about replenishing the earth (Gen. 1:28).

Adam shared with his new wife all that he knew about the Garden of Eden, even the information about the two trees. The tree of life that was available to be eaten from and the tree of the knowledge of good and evil that should not be eaten from. Obeying this simple commandment was the beginning of a great life for the newlyweds.

Chapter Two

They Fall and Could Not Get Up

Everything was moving along nicely until this one particular day. The Mrs. was going out to pick some edibles from the beautiful garden. This was simple enough until she ran into unexpected company. A former angel in heaven with God named Lucifer had now possessed the body of a magnificent creature called a snake. Lucifer had risen with his followers to try a takeover of God's domain (Isa. 14:12–15; Rev. 12:9; Lk. 10:18). Of course, God kicked him and his entourage out of heaven. Now he was doomed never to be redeemed and needed others to share in his misery. This embodiment of the snake could have been Lucifer himself or one of his fallen angels. The enemy, using the serpent, approached the lady and the temptation was on.

Before the creation of our physical world, all existed in a spiritual domain. When Lucifer rose in pride and challenged God for his throne, God got rid of him and all those spiritual beings that agreed to the coup. There was nowhere for them to fall but the second heaven below God's realm or ultimate presence. The earth was made below this space in the universe. The enemies of God, Lucifer and his followers, are now the tempters of men. They can only embody physical beings living on the earth or use thought control of men. Their goal is to distract from God's ultimate plan for man of ruling and reigning over his creation. God's ways are perfect, and his reign is for direction to a perfect existence. This was a point missed by Lucifer and those he convinced to follow him. The enemies' only desire now is to keep man from a peaceful existence with God the creator. The knowledge of this evil in the spiritual realm is what God wanted man to avoid by not eating of the tree of the knowledge of good and evil.

As the Mrs. searched the garden for their next meal, she encountered the snake being used by Lucifer. Of course, she was not afraid because the concept of fear was not part of her makeup (at least not yet). The snake stood face-to-face with her. Unbeknownst to her, this was the enemy, but he was a smooth operator. The enemy was there when God gave Adam instructions and he was also there to hear Adam relay the information to his new wife. He was well aware of the reason behind the commandment, but it was a personal affront to his plans of domination of man against God's design. He would not dare approach Adam, but felt he had a better chance of wooing the one who had received the instructions secondhand. Maybe, by chance, she would get tangled up in thought and words. Oh yes, this was a good plan. Out of all the choices that she had for food, the enemy would trick her into choosing the one forbidden fruit.

Although Satan's name is not mentioned in the creation story or the account of Adam and Eve's demise, it is a known fact from the gospel that Eve (as she would later become to be known) would carry the first child in a line that would produce our savior, the destroyer of the works of the enemy, Jesus. During the writing of Genesis, the concept of evil possession was unknown. Just as new knowledge enhances with each generation, it was no difference in the history of the Bible. Keep reading and in a moment all of this will come together.

The enemy did not waste too many words with the Mrs. He already knew how to twist what she thought she knew to trick her to take the bait. He went about his business convincing the Mrs. of how great this fruit would be to eat. It was beautiful to look at, and it could make you much wiser than you are now. Besides those excellent qualities, the enemy reasoned that God did not want man to eat from this tree because man would end up being just like God and would be God's greatest competitor. Satan knew all about that since getting kicked out of God's domain for attempting the same feat. He knew it was useless, but that was not his plan. He wanted man to have the same plight as him, eventual hell. When the Mrs. started conversing with the enemy, she was already doomed to failure. She is embellishing with words like God told them not to touch the tree. Satan is lying and now she is confused! Satan knew he had her when her memory begins to get fuzzy (then again her husband may have added enforcement by telling her not to even touch *that* tree). The first two humans would take a fall that on their own they would not be able to recover.

The enemy did what he does best: lie. Remember, he had lived with God in heaven before he rose up in pride and wanted to be God. What he told the woman was the same thing he thought while he lived in heaven. He told her that God did not want the humans to be like him. Becoming like God was not even an option since they were already made in his likeness and image. What in the world was missing? This is just a peek into the sin of comparison. Yes, after eating the forbidden fruit, just like God, they would know good from evil, but it would only serve to hinder their perfect walk in the Garden of Eden. Living in a physical world that had the potential for evil would not be properly managed by two humans. God did not equip them to live innocently while maneuvering around the enemy's mess. God wanted them totally dependent on him, which was their best bet. There is no better caregiver than God. The enemy knew this, but had a plan to show them another side. Deception was the only way he could mess up God's perfect creation.

All God wants and always wanted is for man to choose good and forsake the evil. Man had no clue what it felt like to know evil until after eating from the forbidden tree. The forthcoming chain of events would be the beginning of a living death for all humans. No more peaceful existence walking in the cool of the day in the presence of almighty God. The woman picked the fruit from the forbidden tree and ate the fruit, sharing it with Adam who was with her. The humans had succumbed to the enemy's craftiness and disobeyed the only commandment with definite negative consequences. God had planned a beautiful life for the humans, his likeness. Now everything had changed. For all future humans, nothing on this earth would ever be as it was originally planned.

After eating the fruit, the humans were suddenly aware that they were naked. A negative consequence of wrongdoing had instantly entered their sublime atmosphere. All-knowing God knew what happened. Calling out to Adam, he asked where he was. God could see Adam, but wanted Adam to know that he had never left. He gave Adam a chance to confess. That did not happen. When God asked him if he ate from the forbidden tree, his answer was to blame the woman that "he" gave to him. It sounds to me like Adam is trying to make God have some culpability in what he did to himself. When God turned to the woman for an explanation, she followed suit in the blame game, "The devil made me do it!" Don't you know you end up stronger when you can stand up and confess and take your punishment like a man (or a woman). But no, both humans blamed someone or something else for what they had authority to defeat. God did not waste time asking the snake, He already knew what that was all about; he was just up to his old tricks again. Here they stood, God's greatest creation, naked and afraid.

I wonder what would have happened if these two adults had been honest? Honesty is different now than it was back then. They were living in a totally innocent domain, but invited conscience to take over. Before the first sin, humans had absolutely no concept of evil. Today honesty is a chosen character trait. But fantasizing about what could have happened will not change what did happen. These folks not only had to get out of the utopian Garden of Eden, but had to deal with the consequence of sin. God pardons sin, but it results from being contrite, not casting blame. Without inviting Jesus in, the guilt of sin remains with all. The opportunity for repentance is always here. It was in the past and it is now. God has always given man chances to return to him. Even with that, God would later send a savior that only required belief, not previous honesty.

There are many stories of redemption undeserved. King David's story shows me a side of God that has always existed even after the fall of man (read in the book of Psalms and Samuel). Although a confident man, King David lived in humility before God. Confident in whom God created you to be, yet humble enough to know you need God is a character trait that God loves. Pride makes you cast blame on anything but your own failings and still not take responsibility when shortfalls become known to others. King David was an adulterer and attempted to connive his way around his mess. He lay with someone's wife, impregnated her, and then forced the husband off the battlefield so that he could sleep with his wife and it would seem his child. When David's plan failed, he had the man killed in the line of duty. David did all this, but never charged God foolishly. He lived with a godly sorrow that led him to pen beautiful worship in songs found in the book of Psalms. He was grateful for all the mercy shown toward him.

Whether Adam or his wife ever confessed is not written. But you can plainly see the punishment they suffered because it affected all humans born after them. They had consequences coming anyway, but not sure how much different it would have been had they accepted responsibility. In actuality, they cursed themselves. They brought a disruption to their purpose and an end to the promise of eternal life (at least for then). All three defendants were punished. Adam and his wife (Eve, the name Adam gave her after being deposed from the Garden) had excuses, but the serpent was not given an opportunity to defend himself. The enemy had accomplished what he set out to do and most likely thought he'd won. But confession or not, God had a redemption plan already set up for his creation.

God told the serpent that he would crawl on his belly with his face in the dirt for the rest of his life. The second part of the snake's curse had embedded in it a promise for man. "And I will put enmity between thee and the woman, and between thy seed and her seed; it shall bruise thy head, and thou shalt bruise his heel" (Gen. 3:15). What does this mean? Well, the enemy, Satan, is not like God. He cannot be everywhere at the same time. His followers are dispatched to do harm all over the world. This curse was not on a snake but on the one who was using him, the enemy of God, now called Satan (Lk. 10:18).These servants of Satan are considered his seed. They are all spirits; all fallen angels. The seed of the woman are the children she would bear from generation to generation. But this particular seed referenced here is referring to Jesus Christ. Satan's seed would attempt to destroy the future works of Christ, *but* Christ would do greater harm by taking away his power and authority, referenced here as a bruise to the enemy's head. The serpent received his punishment by losing his ability to stand up, and Satan was further brought low by Christ superseding the authority given to him by man's disobedience.

To the woman, God said that she would have children in sorrow. Not only that, but her desire would be to her husband and he would rule over her. There have been many commentaries about this punishment. What did this desire mean? Pain in having and raring children is a given, but desiring her husband does not sound bad. Well, it is when the desire is not reciprocal. You have to remind yourself that these words are wrapped up in a punishment. Even the bruising stated in the punishment for the woman has a positive outcome for humans. The positive outcome in the "desiring" is that the man can get sex as much as he wants from whomever he wants. The result is millions of children with and without fathers in the house! The sorrow of bearing and raising children has not stopped them from entering this world.

My personal belief is that the man does give in, but for the most part when he has something to gain. I refuse to get ahead of myself. This book is about the strength of women and how men can benefit. All sides will be addressed, but not right here and not right now.

The woman has now been doomed to a life of trying to regain her man's attention. After all, she did him wrong. Yes, he opened his mouth, chewed, and swallowed, but he put his trust in her to obey the rules. That did not happen, so now she desires a husband and instead of reciprocation, he dictates her life. Relief will come. But can't you see this set of circumstances being repeated right now. (The why of this book!) It gets better in a while. Some women do everything they can to get a man's attention. They give him much of what he wants, whether he puts a ring on "it" or not. Some are paying all the bills; lying with him even if he is married; and waiting patiently for him to fulfill all the promises that he made. Nothing seems to change, but she keeps repeating the same operation over and over. One man does not work out and she jumps to the next and the next, or lives a life of hopefulness. Then you have couples living the ups and downs of that same ole curse. It is even worse now because she is working too, but many times he is still complaining that she is not doing enough. Or you have the women stuck in the Cinderella syndrome. She wants to quit working and have the man take care of her just as she demands. She is thinking, "Can't you see, I'm desperate. I have kids from the 'sorry' other men and I need some attention." The woman is doing all she can to please her man within the limited confines of her finite mind. What more is there to do?

Most women are not THOTs (those hoes [whores] over there; Urban Dictionary), but they pretend to be to their own detriment. Now there are some real THOTs that can take it. Jumping in and out of the bed does them no harm (at least for the time being). But time catches up to both the fake THOTs and the real ones. It is never a happy ending in this real-life situation. Keep reading and I promise it will get better.

There are women who have resorted to manipulative tactics. That is a whole other story that will be addressed near the end of this book. But not before I get to the godly promises that bring great rewards, not for eternal life off this earth, but for the here and now for those that will adhere to the ways that they were created. It is for the disciplined who will not mind living in principles waiting to be used. It is already built in you to make it better for you. Manipulation is God's job because he created it for himself and not for human use. His manipulation is the definition that says to manage or utilize skillfully. *And*, he does this, causing all things to come together for those working for his purpose.

The man has used his "weapon" for his own gratification, and it sometimes results in the control of women. Then there are the cases of women using their "openings" to draw the man in. With women all possessing the same tools, the man is free to be satisfied all over the world. Some enjoy the game. Some men make it a game of counting women whom they've conquered. But the game never changes, from generation to generation. Life is really not a game, and people do get hurt (men too!). Will you believe me if I told you that it is all a trick to mess up what could be a better existence?

The better life was coming, but men and women had to follow the prepared script. The punishment to the man is what God wanted him to avoid from the start: hard work. Not only would his work now be hard, but the earth would not cooperate. It would bring up thorns and thistles to interrupt the beauty of a plentiful harvest. There was no mention of the man's relation to the woman. God did not even mention to the man that he should rule the woman. He only said that to the woman. The woman was created to help the man. He needed help, but what transpired was disastrous. All over the world women have been relegated to subservient roles. They have had to fight for any semblance of respect. I have found no publicly known religion that dictates the role of women as less than, yet the practice still exists. I just believe that what happened back then dictates the attitudes of now. Men refuse to let history repeat itself (at least they attempt). They subconsciously do not want a woman to lead them down a path of no return. This is a trust issue. Women were created to work side by side with men and to adhere to her abilities of helping him. Men's work is harder than it should be, and women are now fighting to be equal (how ironic). Better had to come!

After the final punishment was distributed, God placed cherubim at the entrance to the Garden of Eden. They carried flames of fire and this blocked reentrance of Adam and Eve after their banishment. This had to happen to keep them from coming in and eating of the tree of life. They lost that right after their disobedience. This is when Adam named his wife, Eve, saying that she was the mother of all living. Why now? Adam had already failed at leadership. He stood and watched his wife being tempted by the enemy and then even sinned with her. Although initially casting blame on God for giving him this woman, he later acts in a repentant way. When his wife was first bought to him, he called her bone of his bone and flesh of his flesh because she was taken out of him. Now standing as a leader in a whole new world, Adam glorifies God by saying that his wife is Eve and the mother of all living. He is picking up the pieces of his authority and leadership outside of the Garden. In many generations to come, Eve's motherhood will include the redemptive son of God, Jesus Christ, Eve's seed that would bruise the head of Satan. No longer in the Garden, this couple would move through the earth and raise children in an altered state.

This altered way of living exists till now, for those who have not yet reclaimed what God has re-established. It is a spiritual reconnection. But it is as close to perfection before moving into the place that is now being prepared (Jn. 14:3). On earth men and women must come into God's forgiveness and govern this sinful flesh so that it does not keep repeating the same errors. Those that subscribe live in a new regenerated near-perfected self. How can anyone do this, since no one is god but God? Made in his likeness and image, you can work to loving yourself and others just like he does. Falling and staying down is then not an option. God fixed this way back then in his second pronouncement over the snake/Satan.

Some women stay home and whine about the kids and their husband's inattentiveness to their needs. Then you have the woman who is all degreed and flaunting her accomplishments to men, only to have them reject all of her fake breasts and butt after enjoying it for a moment. She never developed past her own accomplishments. Most men want the powerful woman, but not the baggage that some carry, including the arrogance. What is really going on? Has wisdom left the building?

The beginning was magnificent, but the enemy's ploy messed up the snake's beauty; the woman turned herself from a powerful helper to a helpless pain; the children are being born in sorrow, and the husband is ruling over the woman psychologically. The man has to forge a living from a ground that has been cursed and now even eating from it is hard. Life is tedious and unfulfilling as man seeks for enjoyment devoid of the original blessings. Many women are longing for the man to love them and treat them like the queen they are supposed to be. Is there any hope for a restart?

Chapter Three

How to Maneuver around the Consequences of Sin and Win

God set you up to win. I want to tell you about a coroneted queen who is going to show you how to make this life work for you. She was not only of strong character, but she knew how to live humbly in a powerful role. God is something else. He joins things together that you must search deep within him to find. The Old Testament holds so many symbols and types that if you are not careful, you will miss the clue to your victory. You must pay close attention because this story from the Old Testament is a key to maneuvering around the consequences of what Adam and Eve invited in by their disobedience. This queen's name is Esther, and her path to victory was the result of listening to those that knew more than her.

Slowly taking you to the steps of being a virtuous woman is the only way for you to become one. (Men, take this in. A man gets involved and his wisdom to the queen ultimately saves an entire race.) Ask any professional person that thrives on other than natural talent; they will tell you that what they possess took time to develop. A medical doctor, a teacher, a lawyer, an executive chef, and even a good wife married for decades had to hone her skills. This is a textbook on the powerfulness of women whose content was lifted right from the pages of what many of you have already read through, the Holy Bible. Each step is moving you closer to what your heart really desires.

This is a script and you are the producer. For years women worked on being what they perceived as the virtuous woman. Some took advantage of opportunities for higher learning. Others hustled their way up the corporate ladder while juggling children, a demanding husband, and extended family requests. Some had a little knowledge of what it meant to be virtuous while others had no knowledge at all. Now you are taking a spiritual course that will promote you to be a top producer of a story that will become number one at the box office called your life.

The biggest part of the virtuous woman remix is the fact that it already exists in you. This is not a new remix. Some women just do not know how it is supposed to work, and men suffer through the process of needing help. The power to live in the story is already here. All you have to do is be willing to either adjust what you already do, replace it, or add to it. It's just that simple.

The period of time you and I live in is called the dispensation of grace. Just like the extra time a teacher may give you to finish a paper or the extra five minutes you take arriving at work without consequences for being tardy. This is the season to be grateful for what God has prepared for you, whether you believe you deserve it or not. Nobody deserves what God does because everybody sins. According to the setup, the pay for sin is death. The previous period, before Christ's death and resurrection, was called Law. That was a time that God proved to every human that they could not possibly obey the entire dos and don'ts. You see if you were guilty of one transgression, you were considered guilty of all of them. There was no use in trying, although many acted as if they abided by every law then judged others caught not obeying. This period of grace is a gift given by way of God's love to make sure everyone is offered the opportunity of an abundant and eternal life with him. Grace is when everyone is blessed to receive what they do not deserve. After grace is a period called Kingdom, and that is the entryway to a permanent life with God where nothing evil will ever live.

You are now entering the world of Queen Esther who lived thousands of years ago. She was both naturally beautiful and virtuous (here meaning extremely useful). She must be included in this discourse because her story exemplifies how God uses grace to free his people. He can fix anything, because he is in control of everything. When it was time, Esther used her authority. God equipped her and set her up. She quickly had to learn how to trust God. Esther is a picture of grace under fire.

The book of Esther is in the Old Testament portion of the Bible. It contains ten short chapters. There are some twists and turns, but the story will point you to an identical strategy of how God always works. God does not neglect to cover himself. He is alpha and omega. He can override any command he gives just by giving another command. You hear people always say that God never changes. This is true, but God regularly adds to what he says. God allows negative circumstances, but then turns and supersedes with a great reward on top of what has already been done. If you read through scripture, you can see God's continued decrees that bring his creation closer and closer to understanding how to fully walk with him while the world around them becomes more depraved. Although the story of Esther is written thousands of years ago, it echoes nuances of how believers can coexist with non-believers, live in abundance right in the middle of the enemy's tactics, and win the battle over lost purpose. The book of Esther is worth the read and works well as a companion to the information on the Virtuous Woman Remix.

Esther is an orphaned Jewish girl being raised by an elder cousin after the death of her parents. Throughout history the Jews lose their way by disobeying God. Chosen as God's representation to a lost and dying world, they were commissioned to live in an altered state of existence than the world around them. God was their provider, but they regularly sought to engage in the evil of the world around them. When they adopted the practices of their neighbors, God would allow them to be defeated in battle and exiled to enemy nations. This story is about one of the times they lived in exile. Esther's uncle Mordecai was a humble leader in a land called Shushan. They lived peacefully up until a day (which happened regularly) they had to don their boxing gloves and fight. From a lowly orphan to a wise queen leading her people to victory in a foreign land is a foreshadowing of current-day believers winning with God's authority.

There came a day when the king of Shushan, Ahasuerus, was having a ball and at the same time in the quarters he allowed her to use, his wife was having her own party. During this ball the king is showing off the greatness of his entire kingdom, even down to the serving utensils. In attendance are all the princes and chamberlains who governed throughout the king's domain. He and his men are drinking and partying. Although, not fully mentioned, I am sure that the queen, Vashti, and her girls are also having a blast.

On the seventh day of the ball, the king is drunk and somewhat full of himself. He has shown all of the finery of his domain except his beautiful wife. He sends one of his boys to bring Queen Vashti from her gathering back to his. He wants her to parade before his male guests wearing only her royal crown (no pun intended). One problem with this fantasy, Vashti refuses to oblige. The king is obviously dejected and unnerved. Something has to be done about her refusal to comply and embarrass the king in front of his admiring audience. This is unheard of that a wife, nevertheless a queen, would disrespect him in front of all his cronies. Strong drink has made his authority take over his character.

Now before you stop reading and make a judgment call, let me explain some things. There is more than one way to do the wrong thing. Ms. Vashti is living in the king's palace and using his extra party room. The king is the boss. Keep in mind that this is not a believing crowd. The Jews are here in exile and do not run anything except their own space. Can Queen Vashti rightfully tell him no to his request? I'll leave that question right there!

One more thing, in a believing house, if a husband asks his wife an outlandish request, what should the wife do? This is going to take some wisdom. God can get believers out of any situation, but they must ask him how. Single, married, or almost there, stop thinking that you can fix every mess up in your life. There is a way out, but your intelligence is not enough to solve every problem.

The king goes from full of himself to being full of remorse for making such a request of his wife in the earshot of all these people. His advisers are making the argument to have Queen Vashti deposed. They want to use Vashti as an example to all the women of the land; these men are concerned that the women will have an uprising protesting the leadership of their husbands. Listening to the men who had his ear, the king succumbed to the pressure. It was decided that Vashti would lose her seat on the throne next to her husband. A decree was put forth and Vashti was removed and it was stated that all women must honor their husbands and allow him leadership of the household. Vashti was out because the king had to save face.

After all of this, throughout the king's domain a decree was sent out to gather all the beautiful virgins so that another queen could be chosen from amongst them. This was not a quick process. The women would have to leave the comforts of their homes and be relegated to the quarters reserved for the king's virgins. While here they would be purified for a year with baths of perfume until each one is called to see if she fit the king's desire for the next queen. All of the young girls not chosen as queen would remain as part of the king's harem. The ladies will never return to their place in society as innocent young girls with lives lived in obscurity.

Mordecai jumped on the opportunity to bring his young cousin, Esther, to such a grand opportunity since he believed that she was so beautiful and of course innocent. He would take her to the gathering in hopes of her possibly becoming the next queen in the palace at Shushan. Mordecai instructed Esther never to mention the fact that she was Jewish. They probably were not ready for that. Let purpose take its course without added information. Her purity and beauty was all that was asked for.

As destiny would have it, from all across the one hundred and twenty-seven provinces under Ahasuerus' domain, Esther was chosen from a field of thousands. After calling for Esther one time, the king was smitten and knew that his choice was clear. Esther, a little Jewish orphan girl, would be the next queen in the palace at Shushan.

Mordecai had risen to the ranks of a government official in the city. One day he overheard two of the king's men planning to assassinate the king. Mordecai made the information known to Esther, who conferred it to the king, vouching for the authenticity of who this reporter was. In the king's record book, a note was made regarding this incident. The two men were hanged and Mordecai went about his daily duties outside of the king's gate.

In the court of King Ahasuerus was a man named Haman. He handled his responsibilities so well that the king promoted him to next in command. With this promotion came the honor of him creating new decrees that had to be followed by all the people of the land. Haman wanted full honor in the community, which included that every citizen bow down when he arrived. Haman was enjoying his newfound notoriety.

The Jews were scattered throughout the land and lived under the guidelines of the Jewish faith. Bowing down to a man was against their belief. There was only one true God and that was who they honored. This seemingly insolent non-action they took while in the presence of Haman was presumed as disrespect. It was a blow to Haman's ego. Up until this point, the Jews had lived peacefully in a land where they were once forced to go after the destruction of their homeland Jerusalem. This quiet cohabitation was about to be disrupted. The king's servants, who dwelled outside the gate along with Mordecai, made it known to Haman that Mordecai would not bow, although he had made it known to them that he was a Jew. In a land where they were strangers, the Jews had previously been allowed to practice their religion without fear of retribution.

This information made Haman furious. He immediately went to the king and asked for additional authority. Realizing that Mordecai was not a man alone in his beliefs, Haman requested to kill all these people that did not obey the king's command. He promised to bring the king ten thousand talents to add to his treasury. Although many have tried to calculate how much ten thousand talents are worth in dollars, there has never been a real estimate. In talents or in dollars, it was an astronomical figure. Haman must have seen the prosperity of the Jews and figured that they would have many valuables in their homes. Haman decided he could have it all confiscated after the genocide/massacre. His power had gone to his head and no one would crush his ego without paying for it with their life.

The king obliged Haman, not even realizing what was really happening. The decree to kill all the Jews was written out and sealed with his ring, meaning that it could not be repealed (remember this point). The letter was sent throughout all the lands where King Ahasuerus ruled. It was slated for a much later date, which meant that the Jews had to live in fear of this terrorist attack until the day that it was carried out. Haman thought he was winning, but he just did not know who he was threatening.

Keep paying attention to how this story is unfolding. Recall that the Jews are believers living in a land that has no reverence for the one true God. That does not matter to God, because he is God and his authority to exact justice is not contingent upon whether someone believes in him or not. His power is even more potent (if possible) when unbelievers are involved (remember this point). God had a plan. God *can* turn the heart of a king (Prov. 21:1).

Queen Esther had not even been made aware of the discussions and actions between her husband, the king, and this evil Haman. Once her cousin found out and it was made known to all the Jews, they wept, fasted, and lay in sackcloth and ashes (a sign of great lament). Mordecai went so far as to come in this condition inside of the king's gate. This was a no-no! Esther heard about this and sent fresh clothes for her cousin, but he refused to put them on. Mordecai wanted a face-to-face talk with his cousin; she had to be made aware of what was going on.

When Esther finally had the opportunity to meet with her cousin, he had a hard request. He pleaded with her to reveal her heritage to the king in hope that he would undo the damage before it could inflict harm on her people. Esther explained that she could not just go into the king's quarters whenever she chose. Even the queen had to be summoned into the king's private space or risk death upon entry, unless the king chose to favor her. Mordecai was paying this excuse no attention; he reasoned that how did she know that God had not set her up in this kingdom just for this opportunity. After much pleading and rebuking, Esther decided that she would listen to her cousin and attempt to save her people and herself from destruction by entering the king's quarters without an invitation.

Esther told Mordecai to put a word out for all Jews to fast three days for her and that she and her attendants would also fast. After that she would go in to the king's quarters, "and if I perish, I perish" (Est. 4:16).

After three days Esther cleaned herself up and most likely put on her best royal apparel to go and meet with the king. She did not know if she would die today or not. It is funny how God operates. Since he has control of the king's heart, why didn't he put something on the king's mind to make him need to see his queen? While she was there, she could have interceded on behalf of her people. But no, God was requiring Esther to live out her faith. What is faith unless it is tested? This is as big as faith can be tested, life or death. Her strengthened faith, undergirded with prayer and fasting, propelled her to step out in the most profound way ever of her entire life.

Contrary to her wildest fears, when Esther went into the king's chambers, she was immediately greeted cordially by her adoring king. The king loved her so dearly that all he asked at this moment was what she desired even if she wanted up to half his kingdom. But all she asked was for him and Haman to attend a banquet that she had prepared. Of course the king did not mind and made sure to tell Haman about the request. The queen was favored and had no trouble getting her man to honor her by accepting her request for attendance at a banquet for him and his assistant. God had entrusted this virtuous woman with wisdom that only he could give. Not only was she interceding for her people, but favor with her man was evident.

In the meantime, Haman was adding fuel to the fire that he had already started. The more he watched Mordecai not fall down at his presence, the angrier he became. When he went home, he called all his friends together and bragged about all of his prosperity and his children. He even told them about the private banquet that he and the king had been invited to. But the main reason he said all of this was to point out the contradiction of his greatness against a lowly believer that thought of him as a mere man. These friends conspired with Haman to kill Mordecai even before the planned massacre. Fueled by Haman's anger, they built gallows so that Mordecai could be hanged. Haman's anger subsided with the thoughts of getting rid of Mordecai once and for all.

During this same time, the king lay awoke one night in his bed. He asked to be brought his records and chronicles so that he could review what had been written. He came across the entry of what Mordecai had done for him some time before (this is reaping what you sow at its best). He asked his servants what had been done for Mordecai for this life-saving deed of reporting the planned assassination. When he was told that the man had never been honored, he started to make plans to do something great for him. He asked for Haman to be brought in. He asked his next-in-charge, without giving a name, what would be fitting reward for a man that had saved his life. As already noted, Haman is puffed up in ego and is very vain. When the king asked about honoring someone who had done him a good service, Haman instantly thought it was him of whom the king was referring. Haman had an excellent idea of how to honor "himself." He proclaimed to the king that the man should put on one of the king's finest garments, the king's ring and crown, and parade "the man" through the city on the horse that usually carries the king. What better way to ensure that everyone knew how much the king honored his second in command? The king sure could sleep well after doing this good deed.

The king loved the idea and told Haman to quickly make all of this happen for Mordecai. Surprisingly revealing that he could fail, Haman ran to his friends crying about this great misfortune. Haman has not seen anything yet. No one ever knows the six degrees of separation. Do you believe if he knew that Mordecai was cousin to the queen his actions would have been the same? Nevertheless, Mordecai, arrayed as Haman had suggested, was paraded through town as Haman cried before him, "This is what is done for the man the king wants to honor" (Est. 6:9 CEV).

All of Haman's friends and his wife seemed a bit wiser than Haman himself. When they heard what had happened, they knew immediately that Haman was in trouble. If this is a Jewish man that seems to be rising higher than Haman, than there is no way for him to win. He is going down (Est. 6:13). Right after they shared their sentiments, Haman was summoned to the banquet prepared by Esther for him and the king.

When they all entered the banquet, no time was wasted on small talk. The king asked Esther what it was that she wanted to discuss. She quickly told of all that had transpired between Haman, Mordecai, and all the Jewish people. It was then that Esther told the king that these people of whom she spoke were all her kindred. The king was enraged and stormed out of the banquet, followed by Esther. Haman followed after her and fell on her bed begging for his life. After all of this activity, one of the king's chamberlains suggested that Haman be hanged on the gallows that Haman had prepared for Mordecai. That was the end of Haman.

There was still another situation to handle. The decree was still in place that would cause all the Jews to be killed. The king's signature along with the seal of his signet ring sealed their fate (Est. 8:8). Compare this decree with the punishment of Adam and Eve in the Garden of Eden. Think of this as a symbol of how God operates. Adam, Eve, and every human born after were doomed to death because of the first transgression. No one can overrule it; if God said it, then it is settled. If God will not change his mind, what can be done? The plight of all humans mirrors the fate of the Jews during Queen Esther's time.

After the death of Haman, Esther knew that the troubles were not over. There was still that decree put in force at Haman's request. Esther was still marching toward her request for the king to do something about this forthcoming disaster. The king explained to Esther that the letters sealed with his ring must stand, but he did have a plan. He would write up another decree allowing the Jews to defend themselves. Remember, they are believers with the hand of God on their lives. How could they lose? Haman's words were headed for the same fate as his life! Death!

King Ahasuerus' command to empower the Jews put fear in the heart of all other people of Shushan. The Jews were celebrating and filled with joy and the previous unbelievers watching in horror. Because they were so afraid, many began to convert to Judaism (Est. 8:17). God's authority wins every time (this is every believer's heritage). After all of this hoopla, it is obvious that the Jews were not defeated as Haman had desired. They went on to greatness.

Mordecai, Esther's cousin, was given a royal place in the king's palace. Every high official of the king's court had helped them win their battle because they were now in fear of who Mordecai had become. All ten sons of Haman had been killed, along with all other enemies. Mordecai was nothing short of the next man in charge to the king. The Jews were now great in the land and went on to live in prosperity.

Did you get the picture? The king did not and could not change what he had decreed, but superseded the first decree with another decree. From being doomed to destruction to being the greatest in the land, the believers' plight had completely turned around. This is a picture of what believers should look like after Jesus' death and resurrection. This is a peep into Kingdom living in the New Testament. You can remain in defeat even with the new order of things, but your faith can propel you to abundant living if you would just subscribe. This is the picture of the lifestyle that God had in mind when he put Esther in the king's house and when he put Jesus on the throne when he ascended after his resurrection. How do you get to this status after being condemned to death? Just like the Jews of Shushan, there is a way out.

The king could not repeal his order, but he could add another order that lessened the effect of the first one. God does not change his commands, but he is God and he *can* supersede a previous order. The payment for sin is still death, but acceptance of Jesus as the sacrificial lamb who died for all is life. The curse was death, but belief in Jesus brought eternal life.

Chapter Four

Her Seed Has Come

It took a powerful woman like Esther to trust God and save a nation. Virtuous does not mean perfect. Virtuous at its core means useful. The righteousness of this virtue is put in place by adherence to the way God designed his creation. Being a helper is more potent than what it appears. Ask any executive assistant, who really runs the CEO's office. Ask a nurse, who keeps the doctor abreast of a patient's care. Ask a long-standing wife, who really keeps the house in order. Esther never usurped authority, but used every tool she could to stay in her purpose; her favor set up an entire nation.

Esther did not just possess beauty, she had poise. Even under pressure, she knew to go to the source, God. She could have finagled a way to get the king to act on her behalf. Jezebel, in the Bible (across 1 Kings 16:31 through 2 Kings), found a way to manipulate an entire court proceeding just to please the covetous desires of her husband, a misdirected king (1 Kings 21:1–29). Esther's composure and love of God made her stay within her purpose and still be victorious.

This is the beginning of why you are reading this book. There is a way to live out life like the queen that resides in every woman. All kings can rest assured that his helper, the queen, is not out to undermine his authority to replace it with her way of living outside of God's intended purpose. Finding how to live in purpose is more satisfying than searching for ways to win using the age-old unyielding pre-established model. If searching for the way to become a true virtuous woman is your ultimate desire, in this chapter you will find the key that God hid within the confines of Eve's punishment.

Some scholars calculate that four thousand years past from creation to when Jesus was born. That is a long time for man to try to get back in right standing with God. But time is in God's hand and there is a time for everything. God is merciful and reminded his creation over and over that they could accomplish nothing without him. In the Bible account of his time on earth, it is said that Jesus walked the earth for thirty-three years before being crucified, his ministry only lasting three of those years. This chapter will be about what Jesus came to do. You may think that it is such a far stretch from creation until four thousand years later, but just like the old song says, "He may not come when *you* want him, but he will be there right on time ("He's an On-Time God," by Dottie Peoples, Charles Fold, Paul Porter)!" Through victories and defeats, God never left. There were other dispensations put in place to draw man close to the dwelling that he left in the Garden of Eden. Jesus' death, burial, and resurrection is the final way of escape before the entrance into an all-spiritual Kingdom with a permanent fellowship between God and man. There may not be another four-thousand-year journey before the dispensation of Kingdom is manifested.

Jesus walked on this earth and gave instructions for living in the Kingdom of God while still on earth. Many believe, yet others refused to believe. His main job was to tell who he was, what he came to do and then be sacrificed for the sins of the entire world (Jn. 3:16). Before that time, innocent bulls and goats were offered up yearly, representing a sacrifice for the sins of the people during the previous year (Heb. 10:2–4). There will never be another animal slain for the sins of anyone; Jesus represented the final sacrifice: an innocent lamb slain so that all people could go free. He walked the earth and Satan bruised his heel everywhere he went (just like prophesied in Genesis 3). But Jesus' final triumph, after being crucified, would be to take away the enemy's authority (Eph. 4:8). This happened after the crucifixion, before he came back to earth in a glorified form and before his final ascension back to heaven to be with his father.

He explained it all and it is recorded in the four gospels found in the New Testament: Matthew, Mark, Luke, and John.

After being raised from the dead, Jesus walked the earth for forty-five days, revealing him to at least 500 people (1 Cor. 15:1–11). He told his disciples to wait for the Holy Spirit that he would send back to earth once arriving and settling in heaven. This gift would be sent seven to ten days after Jesus' return to heaven (Acts 1). The Holy Spirit would enable man to stand under the pressure of the enemy that lurked all around. Man would have more power to control his spirit than ever existed before. Jesus' last walk on earth was for final instructions for all that followed him and further instructions on inviting other followers.

This is the key to combatting temptation that is always being planted in the thoughts of all men and women. You can live in this sin-filled world and still not RSVP to the invitations that lead to death to purpose. God sent Jesus to redeem all people from the curse. Although once given the opportunity to eat from the tree of life that was also in the Garden of Eden, Adam and Eve were kicked out before they could. Eternal life was restored after Jesus' death, burial, and resurrection. "For God so loved the world, that he gave his only begotten Son, that whosoever believeth in him should not perish, but have everlasting life" (Jn. 3:16). Yes, the enemy still tempts God's creation, but for every temptation, there is a way of escape (1 Cor. 10:13). God always wanted man to be able to live forever. He is an eternal father and wants his children with him forever. Not only has God restored eternal life, but his son returned abundant life for those that would believe (Jn. 10:10).

Because of Adam's indiscretion, sin came to everyone after him. Why through Adam? Remember, the commandment was given directly to him before Eve existed. After the introduction of sin, everyone was doomed to death. Just like sin came on you as a consequence of being human, Jesus' free gift is also available to you. "By one man sin (Adam) entered into the world, and death by sin; and so death passed upon all men, for that all have sinned:" (Rom. 5:12). 1 Corinthians 15:45 refers to Jesus as the second Adam. Jesus accomplished what Adam could not do, retain abundant and eternal life. The power of Christ's Holy Spirit is how Satan's head is bruised. A head injury is incapacitating. Jesus was the replacement of a flawed sinful man (Adam) and for this everyone gets a do-over.

Are you still not convinced of your authority to deny Satan what he wants? Sin is only sin if there is a law against a particular offense. What really happened was that death took over from Adam's sin until Moses and the law that came from God. As an unbelieving human, you are walking in a dead state, like the walking dead. Real life comes from God. Everyone died after Adam and Eve ate from the forbidden tree. (God cannot lie). Besides what the Word says, you know how life feels without the Holy Spirit guiding your life from the inside. Then from Moses to Jesus, people lived to the best of their *own* ability struggling to comply yet still transgressing the law which is sin. The dispensation or time period of Law started with the Law given to Moses. God continued to think of man in every dispensation. He kept calling man back to him. Some were able to embrace God's truth and submit to his authority, but never fully. Throughout history there are those left as witnesses (Heb. 12:1). Adam's offense made everyone born a sinner; Jesus' blood on the cross covered all men from Adam until what will be the end of what is called time. He is the final sacrifice (Rom. 5:12–14 and Heb. 10:26). There is nothing left for you to wait for to overcome the curse. Jesus won for you the right to live as God originally designed. You cannot do it alone, but must embrace the empowering force of the Holy Spirit.

Let us bring the last paragraph home for the virtuous woman. Eve listened to the enemy and believed his lies about operating just like God. Because of this, all women have operated in an altered purpose: Making babies in anguish, longing for the love of a man, and fighting against the man's rule over them. Many women deny having all of these issues. Some have had no children, but they do have a cycle every month until old enough not to. Whether they admit it or not, many women have a deep desire to have a man who cherishes them and calls them queen. Finally the battle of the sexes keeps the women at odds with men, who perceptually want to rule them. She disobeyed her husband in the Garden and now her conscience would make her live in constant trepidation of his correction. He listened to her, yet still blames her for listening to the snake. Can she ever do anything perfectly? Doing wrong at the beginning destroyed innocence. That wrong was then converted to sin after Law came onto the scene through Moses. Sin was then sent packing after Jesus took the punishment for sin by dying on the cross. The re-established purpose is available to those that will take on the power intrinsic in the Holy Spirit.

This brings you back to what this book is talking about. Throughout the scripture, it is revealed how God made ways for people to escape from all the consequences of wrongdoing and return to a peaceful existence with him. This claim is reiterated in Romans 6:23, "For the wages of sin is death, but the gift of God is eternal life through Jesus Christ our Lord." This was the price of wrongdoing from the beginning and continues to be, but Christ paid the debt for everyone with his death on the cross. The way back to God is through Christ.

Anyone can deny Christ; that does not make him any less real. No one can deny the reality of the disruption of peace between men and women. The war still rages on today. In most love relationships, women do not know how to use their God-given ability for success and men do not know how to appreciate a woman who does. But there is a way to escape this oxymoron. The woman who has tapped into her divine purpose through Christ should remain there and not waiver no matter who promises what. If she does not yet have a man, she will still prosper and the one who finds her will greatly benefit. "Whoso findeth a wife findeth a good thing, and obtaineth favour of the Lord" (Prov. 18:22). God enabled women to be wives without a husband, so that the man is looking for his wife before she has his name. This passage is from the Old Testament, and the power to fulfill it comes with the power of Christ's spirit and to those who were graced to tap in long ago.

When Christ died on the cross and rose again, he snatched the power of death, hell, and the grave and rendered the devil powerless on the earth (Eph. 4:9 and Rev. 1:18). You probably wonder how Satan continues to operate on the earth. He still exists. He runs the airway right above your head (Eph. 2:2). As a spirit, he listens to every word that is spoken and uses it against anyone that allows him. He also has the ability to ask God if he can tempt a child of God (this is referenced in the book of Job and the story of Job's life found in the Old Testament). There is power in words. God created the entire universe with the authority of his word. Satan mocks God and merely suggests things to people. People carry out his bidding on the earth. Your authority over the negative comes from having the mind of Christ. You must make every thought obey what Christ promised that would come through Kingdom living (1 Cor. 10:5). This will automatically snatch away the enemy's power to operate against your life on the earth

You are made free by what Christ did for you. Acts 1:8 declares that you will have power once you receive the gift of the Holy Spirit. Acts 2:38 says to repent and then get baptized and you automatically receive the free gift of the Holy Spirit. Your freedom is guaranteed and you then have the authority to walk around a sinful world, yet be covered by this cloak of righteousness. Letting Christ abide in your life gives you discipline over your flesh. The flesh is what failed Adam and Eve in the Garden. You get eternal life by believing, and you get abundant life on earth by allowing Jesus to live in you and direct your life. The answer to your freedom is asking for direction in every area of your life, through prayer, asking someone wiser than you and knowing what he says in the bible.

God is so awesome that he put in the Old Testament a way to live virtuously here in this century. Some did well, yet others did not. Now the gift is free for all. This is as perfect as it can get until living in the future in a new earth that is being prepared for all believers. (Rev. 21:1). This is the life that God intended when he created you. This is now the beginning of the remix. The next chapter will give you specific instructions on how to operate in this new life and how to let it work for you.

Chapter Five

What Is She Really Created to Do?

Have you ever noticed that the Gideon Bibles that you can find placed in rooms at hotels not only contain the entire New Testament, but also include Psalms and Proverbs from the Old Testament? I wondered why. I went to my trusty Google search and found that the Gideons are a group of business and professional believers wanting to encourage people to read the Word of God. They wanted to get right to the point of salvation for all that would believe without having them try to decipher the background information found in the Old Testament. Psalms and Proverbs are included because Psalms is full of encouragement and Proverbs is written by those walking in wisdom. Now I see another reason for Proverbs being included. The last chapter lists the attributes of a virtuous woman. That's one answer for Proverbs being included with a Bible containing 100 percent New Testament.

This earth will never again return to its former glory. The perfection of the original creation is forever marred. But living inside God's Kingdom on earth is just a small step closer to God's complete rule in your life and the peace that he has always promised. Just like in Esther, it is the believer's job to point others to the escape route of the destruction that is all around.

Living in God's Kingdom on earth is the only hope for a better life. Other than that, it is living to fight the consequences of the curse brought on by the first sin committed by humans. Why am I writing all of this? If you cannot renew your mind to this Kingdom living, then hearing about the operations of a virtuous woman found in Proverbs 31 is useless. In your carnal or fleshy mind, you will rebel against the principles and feel that you can find a better way. Well, I'll ask you right now before you read any further, how has living outside of God's Kingdom on earth been working for you?

Connecting to your love interest is just as important as loving your neighbor. It is so easy to think that the foundation of compassion to be shown to others is sometimes neglected when it comes to the opposite sex who happens to be a spouse, lover, or love interest. These are people too. It is so easy to take advantage of a relationship after you have been in it a while or when the love interest has shown you authenticity. There is one law to consider when it comes to this: the law of reciprocity.

The platform of the virtuous woman is what God had established at the beginning of time and that was the relationship between God and human and then man to woman and woman to man. God gave what he expected in return: love and respect. He related lovingly to his creation, and they in turn related lovingly to him and then toward each other. This perfection was broken when the humans forgot how to treat God. Just like counselors and wise people offer, you have to teach others how to treat you. When this rule is violated, everything else runs haywire. Relationship is based on how you treat others and in return how they treat you. It is not more prevalent than in a love relationship when the goal is permanence.

The virtuous woman is first about how a woman is to develop in her purpose for being on this earth and secondly how a wife is to relate to her husband in every area of her life. There is no confusion of roles or purpose and what she does compliments her husband's role in her life and his and her place in society. Some folks get it all twisted. The desperation to have a mate makes people put the cart before the horse. How is he supposed to pull it if it is in front of him? Work on loving yourself first and building good relationships in every matter. First your relationship with God, then the great one you have with yourself, thirdly those around you, including family and neighbors, and finally that intimate one with your significant other. If you practice developing the first four, the last one will not carry as much weight. The last one is not eternal, but the others are (Matt. 20:30).

The virtuous woman's place alongside her husband is secure as long as this relationship is put in the proper perspective with the symbolism of marriage representing the Kingdom of God (Eph. 5:25–33).

There are so many educated and powerful women in executive positions that describing this reality with how it relates to having a man must be explained. Whether there is a woman who is not in a rush to the altar or the one desperate to be married, there is a place for being virtuous. She may have a doctorate or be a high school dropout; there are only a tiny percentage of women who do not want any kind of love relationship. But the advent of the high-maintenance woman can be a place of difficulty in a relationship if the woman does not know how to handle her advantage. Maintaining her own high level of living is a part of being a virtuous woman. It cannot be at the expense of a spouse or children suffering. But if you *and* your spouse can agree to a status of life, then do it! You cannot force it on a man. Virtuosity is a useful tool. Having a six-figure income is no guarantee of being virtuous. Any asset has its proper place. No matter your status, you can win.

It is so unfair how some women wield their ingenuity in making a household grand in an unwise fashion. If you have a man who is very conscious about what is going on in your world, you cannot just do things at home or in your life without including him in the conversation. You and your girl are going to take a ninety-day cruise around the world. You announce to your husband that the kids will be taken care of by the nanny and you are leaving in seven days. Unless you and your man are like two ships passing in the night, this could spell trouble. Suppose he wants to go but never was made aware of the plans? Or suppose he had a surprise for you in thirty days and now must change them. I do not care how much expendable time and cash you have, proper communications is always a must if you are married. Money may answer things, but it does not answer a heart. You may think that your husband should be proud that you can make these kind of plans on your own, but this does not spell out usefulness to a man that is fully involved in what you do. You must employ wisdom.

It does not matter if you have a gigantic business deal that will benefit the whole household, some men will not subscribe to you making big decisions that will affect him without his knowledge. Learn the ways of your spouse and make it a practice to do better the next time after a big blowup. Some women, under the umbrella of being virtuous, think that their independence is key to the good life. No, your independence is only favorable when it fits into his dependence on your independence. You cannot use your independence to control him. Upgrading the house, taking family vacations, buying a new car, or having the carpet cleaned will benefit everyone; why not skillfully include him so that he feels like it was both your decision?

When dating, it is especially advantageous for a woman to watch what she reveals about her assets. A woman who knows how to maneuver through the economic ups and downs is an asset. The biggest problem is with attitude. Whether a man wishes for a "made" (financially affluent) woman or not, she cannot flaunt that as her opening act. If a man wants a woman, he does not want a "man/woman" who wants a man, but flaunts how much she's just like him. Oh, you will get a man, but he may just want what you have. See how long this lasts. Some even marry for your money, but that is exactly what you will get. This is not the description of a virtuous woman. It is a paced existence, with both the man and the woman in a partnership. What the virtuous woman does and what she has will come into play, but might never if she starts off with the presentations of all her assets. In most surveys it has been revealed that men want a woman who brings something to the table, but do you want a man that only wants you because you have financial assets? What you bring to the table cannot be your net worth and that is it. Knowing your worth in all areas of life is your greatest addition.

There are so many dimensions to women, but knowing what God created her to be is the key to living in success. Whether you have a man or not, you can stay ready to enjoy the company of a man that needs a woman like you. You do not have to flaunt what you are supposed to be doing anyway. Remember, God created women for men, but a man wants to know that you need *him*. If a man feels like you are just in it for what he can offer, that will leave him feeling empty. No matter your status in life, knowing how to handle your purpose is a big plus.

Flaunting how useful you are to society is not a come-on. When you sit down with a potential suitor, be confident but not arrogant. If he lets you lead the conversation, then interview him. I have heard about all those women who take his quietness to mean he wants to hear about all your accomplishments. I guarantee this is wrong. Start the interview and if he wants to know about you, he will ask. I know this sounds archaic, but I promise it will work. Just because you may have led the conversation does not mean you have to be the center of it!

When I first began studying and writing on this subject in 2009, the dilemma of the successful woman trying to balance career with love life stood bright in my mind. Women complained of the men that wanted attention that she "did not have the time to give" or the man who exhibited jealously of her seemingly fast move to the top of her career. Way back then a picture came to my mind. It was of Joyce and Dave Meyer. Joyce Meyer is the engine that affords Joyce Meyer Ministries' business all the fringe benefits. Dave Meyer runs the business and other family members hold positions in this world-renowned ministry. Of course I do not know Joyce or Dave personally, but from what I can see and what I've read, their setup has run successfully for decades. If you have ever heard Joyce Meyer speak or read any of her books, you can see the balance of her originality mixed with godly wisdom that has propelled Dave and the family to the "class A" ministry that they comprise. She has nothing but complimentary words for her husband. On television, when the camera cuts to Dave's face, his eyes look adoring and appreciative to his beautiful wife. She tells of her humble and abusive beginnings and how Dave saw her potential and encouraged her rise to where she stands today. Now that is God gluing real manhood and a virtuous woman together like only he can.

Men are supposed to be finding a wife. To be a wife you must have worked on some things. Whether you ever get married or not, you can be that great wife that is an example of a real virtuous woman. If you want a man, then you must live in the status of a wife because that is what he is supposed to be looking for (Prov. 18:22). There are some women who have been raised by a virtuous woman who trained them well, but there are some who passed down bad advice because they really did not know some things. As a result many have been ill-equipped to handle a husband or the responsibility of running a household. It is never too late to develop in the areas where you are weak as a wife.

I have sat and coached women who thought they were supposed to "mother" their men. They do not understand why their spouses despise them. They buy and pick out his clothes, wake him up for work, make him eat vegetables, and tell him he needs to take more baths. Instead of curtailing this activity, some men just allow her to nag, but spend more time away from home or in "his cave." She has no clue why he is acting this way. Just think about a teenage boy after he starts dating. Mother begins to be less of an attraction. You now have a "son" (translated: husband) that will never mature if you never stop acting like "mommy."

Believe me, I have seen men benefit from the overaggressive woman, but deep inside it grates on their nerves. The most docile men will rebel through extracurricular affairs or quietly denying her wishes. The benefits do not outweigh the real desires. Men really want an equal, someone they can depend on for companionship and help, but not one who takes over at every turn.

I know two women on opposite ends of the spectrum when it comes to the purpose of a husband. Both of them come from a single-parent household. One mother told her daughter that you cannot do anything without a man although she raised her without the benefit of a man in the house. The daughter fought this information psychologically while systematically destroying a good marriage. She was rebelling against her mother's words while battling the fact that she subconsciously married a man that wanted to take care of her. The other woman was told that she did not need a man to succeed. She has been fighting off her husband's attempts to help her in any area that he may be better suited to handle. Neither one of these mothers' statements was true, but most likely came from women who only guessed at virtuousness and passed the misinformation down to their daughters. Being married can be balanced if founded on godly truths from both spouses. Both of these women could have adjusted what they thought to match what God said and things would have come out differently,

Although Proverbs 31 is in the Old Testament, its precepts are everlasting and universal because they are written in wisdom. Every society has a purpose for all its inhabitants. For the women living in the inner cities of the United States, they may not go out to meet ships that bring goods from afar, but they may shop at international markets that carry the goods bought from other countries by way of merchant ships. The description of the virtuous woman found in Proverbs 31 can be picked up and placed in the twenty-first century and yet still make sense.

Read this chapter with an open mind. Even if you have never heard this teaching before, does not mean that it has no place in your life? You can already be doing great without the knowledge of the virtuous woman. Can you imagine how it would feel if you add God's perfect design to your life? I remember a lady came to our ministry and became offended by something that the pastor read from scripture about tithing. She waited around long after service was over so that she could privately talk to the pastor. Since the pastor's wife had already gone for the day, the pastor asked me to hang around so that he would not be alone with her. She began complaining that her children were disturbed by the passage in Malachi that said that man would be cursed with a curse for withholding their tithes and offering. She said that she was blessed although she had never paid her tithes. This chapter has nothing to do with tithing or offerings, but the point of this story is to tell you that even if you are already doing well, you can still add enhancements from the virtuous woman. Nobody knows or does it all. That is exactly what my pastor told the lady that wanted to reject truths found in the scripture. If she was doing so well without giving the Bible way, just think how much greater she can do if she does. Open your hearts and minds and add to your repertoire of victorious living.

This book in the Bible is written by a wise king quoting the instructions told to him by his mother. Yes, the virtuous woman chapter is written by a man that listened to his mother. Some scholars believe that King Lemuel is another name for King Solomon, the wisest king that ever lived. Whatever the case, this king's mother knew how to direct a great man. She starts very early by telling him not to give his strength to women (Prov. 31:3). This particular verse came alive for me about twenty years ago. When I was attending many church services alone with my two sons, a lady stopped me after Sunday service one day to inquire of my spiritual connection to my husband. Specifically she wanted to know if he and I ever prayed or read the Bible together. I told her that we had not and she suggested I ask him about reading the Bible with me. Upon my arrival home, the kids went their way and I entered my bedroom, where my husband was lounging. I asked if we could read a scripture together. He lightly shrugged a mixed reaction. Then I offered that he could open the Bible and whatever verse he saw, that is what we would read. He obliged. This is when I found out that this King Lemuel's mother knew what she was talking about.

Proverbs 31:3: "*Give not thy strength unto women, nor thy ways to that which destroyeth kings.*"

My husband opened the Bible and it fell to Proverbs 31:3: "Give not thy strength unto women." He closed the Bible and we both laughed. We have never again read the Bible together. I cannot manage his relationship with God and neither can anyone manage mine. Proverbs 31 is filled with these kinds of principles, but mostly directed at the kind of queen/wife that this king should look for. Note here that you are a queen. You do not have to be coroneted for it to be official. The description of the virtuous woman found in this chapter in Proverbs was written by a mother instructing her son on what to look for in a queen. It is no different for you. How can he be the king of the house and you are only a lowly servant? That does not make sense. When he acts like a king, put your crown on. The words in Proverbs 31 would resonate with a wise man that submitted to the sentiments of his wise mother. This is how to remain strong as a man *and* it is how a strong woman knows how to live out her purpose with a strong man while she maintains her own strength.

I have heard over the years that the description of a virtuous woman found in Proverbs 31 could not be the assets of one woman. Then there is the incidence of her having handmaidens. This did not faze me, a girl who grew up in the largest housing development in the United States, Queensbridge Housing Projects in New York City. The handmaidens are not mentioned to boast of how wealthy she has to be, but of course the description is for the wife of a king. I see myself as the queen of my home. Why can't a woman operate as a queen of her domain? You want to marry a king? You will be a queen. For the record, I believe that one woman can encompass all of these attributes.

Proverbs 31:10: "*Who can find a virtuous woman? For her price is far above rubies.*"

The first description of a good woman starts in Proverbs 31:10. Her worth is greater than rubies. Now I know that there is a saying that diamonds are supposed to be a girl's best friend, but rubies are just as precious as diamonds. In the right cut, they can be worth a higher price.

The average price of a one-carat ruby is $10,000–$18,000; the average price of a one-carat diamond is $3,500–$26,000 (www.Bluenile.com). Compare me with a perfect gemstone; I will take that. It says that you are worth more than that. The next verse says that the husband's heart safely trusts her and he does not have to fight his way to being prosperous. This is truly amazing since Psalms 118:8 says that it makes more sense to trust God than to put confidence in people. But if a man can find a woman whose worth is greater than rubies, I am positive that God put that in her. You can trust that. When you consistently can be trusted to come through for what blesses the household, how can your man not savor that?

Proverbs 31:11–12: "The heart of her husband doth safely trust in her, so that he shall have no need of spoil. She will do him good and not evil all the days of her life."

A great woman will make a good man not have to work so hard. With all the hard work that powerful men put in, I have been around so many of them that say that if it were not for the draw of a good woman that their desires would be much smaller. Proverbs 31:11 alludes to this: A man who has a strong work ethic is blessed with less stress if he has a woman full of great character and wisdom.

She will not waste his money and lives with excellent stewardship principles.

All of the talk from women who want to get back at the man who did them wrong has another side to it. If you ever have a talk with some of these women, you would find some interesting stories. There is the case of the woman who lived with her lover and then had a child. They break up and he is ordered to pay child support. She works but soon finds herself without a car. Her ex-boyfriend has two cars, one his work truck and the other for leisure. The only problem is that this leisure vehicle has a note on it. He is willing to allow her to use it if she can manage the payment. She runs around complaining that the car payment is the same amount as his child support check. It just happens that it is close to the same amount (she makes the payment directly to the bank). This woman plans to muddy her ex-boyfriend's name as much as she can and accept no culpability in her life's current situation. Although she may not have known better, she moved in with a man without the benefit of some papers and now she thinks that because she has a child that he is supposed to support the lifestyle that *she* wants. Can you find any virtue in that? If you are a woman given to negative thoughts of men, take your time and reread the above story with a different perspective. It is always good to take some responsibility in what happens to you, so that you will not go through life always living like you will always be a victim to the whims of other people. Sure, her baby's daddy could have let her use his car for free, but that is his choice whether or not to do that. God has given you more authority over your life than that. I sure hope someone found her, maybe someone like a life coach. Being a virtuous woman is all about self-sufficiency in what God created you to be. You can go around and demand things from people; that is your right. But whether or not someone serves you as they should plays no part in God's benevolent care for you through your own God-given abilities. There was really no real fight for this lady; just a waste of time playing victim.

As a believer, you must tap into this virtuous way of thinking. You can justify any stance that you take in the game of life. Some stands are such a waste of time. I would rather find an answer in God's Kingdom and share it with those who desire real change. If a man will not take care of his child, take him to court. But having babies with love interest has no legal bearing on him taking care of you and the baby. This way of thinking goes against the grain of the foundation of being virtuous (useful).

It would be good at this point to talk about what virtue is. According to the Merriam Webster Dictionary, virtue is a person of good moral character. The biblical definition is much the same, except it adds words like uprightness and chastity. It is actually not something hard to live up to, that is if you want to. None of this is mandatory, but it will work if you reconcile your life to its principles. Who would not want to be a woman described as powerful as a man, yet tender as a woman? Virtuous as a woman describes a woman who can stroke her man's ego while changing a tire! She can fix her man's dinner while laying carpet in her lady den!

> ***Proverbs 31:13–16: "She seeketh wool, flax, and worketh willingly with her hands. She is like the merchants ships; she bringeth her food from afar, she riseth also while it is yet night, and giveth meat to her household, and a***

portion to her maidens. She considers a field, and buys it: with the fruit of her hands she plants a vineyard."

This woman is busy and proves to be quite industrious. Now, do not think that all women have to do all these things. God equipped you to do it all, but there are men out there that may not want all that. My mother was of Jamaican heritage and grew up on that country's cuisine. My dad was from deep South Georgia and loved the rich food of that area. None of us knew my mom could cook until our father got sick and did not have the strength to stand for hours in the kitchen. They both had us fooled. I believe he just wanted soul food and that was not her specialty, so she yielded the kitchen to her man. I remember very few of my mother's offerings. I was raised with a nightly plate running over with rice and gravy, fried fish, corn bread, and collard greens. No, we did not have the same meal every night, but it sure was soul food that we had to wait up late to eat. My mother was virtuous, and the older siblings tasted peas (really beans) and rice while visiting after getting married and leaving home. The virtuous woman knows her purpose and is content to fit in where needed. This sometimes takes time to discover. You must be patient. My mother's industrious ways gave her a full-time job on a second shift, washing and pressing her girls' hair on Saturdays, and finally introducing her cooking skills when Daddy got tired.

When my sisters and I were growing up, my mom could sew. She had an old Singer sewing machine and made some of our clothes. Then my oldest sister and I, the next to oldest, also learned the trade. Early in my marriage, I made every outfit that I wore, including all my maternity wear. That flax that the above passage mentioned is the plant that makes linen. In Bible times, flax was the most important plant fiber. Ever bought a fine linen suit? Well, that is what most clothes were made of in the Bible days. If someone is a good seamstress, their clothes can fit better and can be of better quality because saving money is a huge part of being virtuous. My mother taught her daughters well.

Not only did the virtuous woman buy things to create fashion, but she also cooked exotic food after meeting ships at port coming from foreign lands. Now, you do not have to go to the port to buy crab or octopus, but you sure can go to international markets that are housed throughout cities all over. He does not want noodles, hotdogs, hamburger, rice, or spaghetti from a can as a regular diet. He also may not be happy that you are feeding this to the kids. Anyone can cry poor, but any food is expensive when you do not manage your funds correctly. A pack of chicken leg quarters can go a long way if you do not think of this as just thighs and legs. Okay, I am not going to give a cooking lesson here because that is *not* my forte. Being creative is only a portion of the virtuous woman's day. There is still more.

There is no place for laziness. If that is you, just say "ouch." Much of what many women complain about is things that require her to work a little harder. But when you are virtuous, the work is not tedious. I used to love coming home from my nine-to-five and putting together a balanced meal. It wasn't until my son told a story at a youth service that included the statement that he thought fried chicken was supposed to be black that I realized he knew differently about my "excellent" cooking skills. I did laugh, but it just woke me up to the fact that my son knew one of my handicaps. There is, however, a story of my ingenuity in the kitchen that has nothing to do with laziness, but everything to do with ignorance!

Back in my dating days, I invited a young man over for dinner one night. I had bought a whole chicken (something I had always seen my dad do) and I cut it up to the best of my ability. The thigh piece looked pretty decent. I bought some oil and floured and seasoned my meat. When it had finished frying, that piece looked like it was ready for a commercial. I made greens and mashed potatoes. The young man came over and we sat down to eat. When he had gotten past the crispy skin, he bit into a part that was as pink as my tongue. The chicken was not done. I apologized and we ate the greens and mashed potatoes. The motto of the story is: don't practice a skill on a love interest; practice on yourself first.

After raising two kids and a husband on "darkened" fried chicken, I now fry it and then put it in the oven on low to let it finish cooking. My husband tells me to cut into it to check if it's done. I still feel virtuous because I have never quit and still regularly cook for my husband of forty years.

The best lesson I was ever taught was directly from an angel. Cooking breakfast every weekend is one of my passions. I bring it to my husband on a tray while he is still asleep. One Friday night, we had a huge disagreement. As scripture says, you should never go to bed angry (Ephesians 4:26), but this time I failed. This guideline is not just for marriage but all relationships, but I just could not get it together this night. On Saturday morning, I was still mad. In an hour, ten ladies would be coming over for a book club reading. I did not want to cook breakfast for this man that had made me feel this bad. As I began to get dressed, I heard the voice of Jesus say, "Cook breakfast for me this morning." I obliged and that was probably the best-looking breakfast that my husband had ever seen. Since that day, I have upgraded all my food tray entries. For me, I am the room service attendant to my husband as if we are in a five-star hotel. Thank you, Lord, for the lesson. I believe it blesses me more than it blesses my husband. My hands are anointed to do what God blesses me to do.

Let me add a disclaimer. I can cook, but my taste is not for soul food. I love the short orders. That is why as we got older, my father only gave me about two turns to cook for the family. As everyone sat down to eat looking at a plate with four "fake" Jamaican meat patties and some salad just made those six other family members mad (especially my "big man" dad).

Proverbs 31 talks about this great woman working with her hands and she seems to enjoy every minute of it. What happened to all of this creativity? Creation is a lost art in many women's homes. I actually prefer my designs to some that I see. I remember covering some captain's chairs with covers that I made by hand. It was not that I could not afford covers, but I just wanted to create some. These same sturdy chairs still stand in my dining room and they are now covered with store-bought designs this time. Do I *have* to buy brand-new chairs every time I need a different color? I love the work of my hands. I know you can do something creative with your hands. (Maybe you already do!)

I hear more about gardens being planted than I ever have before. This virtuous woman bought land and planted a vineyard. Many of you own land and some are growing vegetables. You do not have to own land to have a garden! A windowsill garden in an apartment can yield all kinds of vegetation: peppers, tomatoes, strawberries, etc. Every year, I am working on this venture. So far in ten years, I have grown a cherry tomato and one strawberry. No exaggeration!!! However, the house is covered with houseplants. Thank you!!! I have not given up though; every year, I try again. So far this year, I see a one-eighth inch green tomato trying to grow. I hope he tells his siblings that I'm good ground! I'm not thinking about organic; I just want a garden.

The virtuous woman is not only industrious, but she starts her day early in the morning. She is not chasing money, but she is redeeming time. I have learned that redeeming time is the way to being financially blessed. You never know what will prosper you until it prospers you. I remember making women's oblong ties to wear with button-down blouses when this was in style in the early eighties. I worked in the bank, so you saw many scarves like this matching suits that were comparable to the ties that men were wearing. To sell them to my coworkers, I would stay up late and wake up early to make them. I do not believe that I was thinking virtuous at the time, but I guess it was. One yard of fabric could make up to seven of these scarves. My average was about a 30 percent return on investment. Not bad!

Proverbs 31:20: "She stretches out her hand to the poor; yea, she reaches forth her hands to the needy."

No matter what your status in life is, if you think of what you can do for others, you will always have more. I work to help everyone that will let me. When I was growing up, I had never heard that prosperity or poverty is not measured in dollars and cents. While still living with a poverty mindset that told me that I had to work harder in order to prosper, I reached out my hand to help everyone I thought could use the help. My father taught me that. And of course there were those that perceived that I was doing better than they were, so that hands were often outstretched (that's ok, but its states that the virtuous woman stretches out her hands). I had to have help in this area. But I benefitted from giving to as many as I could. This is all pre-virtuous realization and way before being taught about living with a Kingdom of God mindset that teaches that God is the source of all my supply. I wanted to help, but needed more teaching on living out a prosperous life.

Being prosperous was an attitude I learned after moving to Georgia. At the time, my pastor, Rogers Murray, was teaching about the Kingdom of God here on earth. That is when I learned that prosperity is not measured in dollars and cents. It is a realization that God is the source. The Kingdom of God cannot be seen with the natural eye (Luke 17:20). Knowledge of the Kingdom of God is revealed in the spiritual realm. This remix of the virtuous woman story is about living a life of prosperity made available by the death, burial, and resurrection of Jesus (John 10:10).

Prosperous people find it very easy to share the blessings that they have because prosperity is depending on God to increase the work of your hands, and poverty is dependence on systems and people to give to you.

Proverbs 31:21: "She is not afraid of the snow for her household; for all her household are clothed with scarlet."

Scarlet was the name of fabric that kept people warm. The virtuous woman is a shrewd businesswoman and plans for the unseen. In Proverbs 22:3, it tells of a wise person who sees evil and plans, in contrast to the unwise that moves on with no thought for tomorrow and they are punished. With an eye on the future, there are times of unexpected expenses that can happen to every family. Planning diminishes fear. Some have mistakenly believed that planning for tomorrow is worrying. They are two separate entities. One can strike out the other. The wise woman creates a peaceful panic-free atmosphere for her entire family by having several plans, just in case. I have heard many people say that with faith, all you need is one plan. Well, according to my faith, I want a winter coat, an electric blanket, and several area heaters just in case the pilot light goes out in the middle of the night.

Early in my marriage, I had to maneuver through my husband's lack of knowledge of my budgeting skills. It is my belief that a unified vision on the household finances brings more peace to a home than anything else (of course, this comes after God being at the center). I have had a budget since my first job at fifteen or maybe even before while selling Avon at age twelve. After marrying, I created a budget that included my husband's income. Being on his own since he was seventeen, this was nearly ten years later when we started a joint venture. Yes, a household is a business. Going from a single man to having a wife and son, he was not quite ready to commingle. That is understandable because he did not even know if he could trust me in this area. We have always had two separate accounts. He was not really reluctant, but would sometimes give me varying amounts each week. I kept trying to explain to him that the budget called for a certain amount and this was not working. Then *I* changed. I noticed a trend in his spending habits. I began to change the budget to account for these incidentals. Unlike some women who will not bend, I listened to what I have been told that some men want cash in their pockets. My budgeting skills needed some tweaking. Forty years in and the budget is nearly perfect. We discuss upcoming events, budget for vacations, and when we desire, make donations outside of our tithing and offering. This working-in-tandem thing really works when the woman can show that she means her man no harm.

> ***Proverbs 31:23: "Her husband is known in the gates, when he sits among the elders of the land."***

The woman who takes care of her household makes her husband have a better life. He should not see his wife as a big bill lying beside him. Don't take that too personally because some men can afford to take care of three families if they had to. A better life is not just about money either. My husband attends church service, but not every time the doors open. I love attending like that, but not at the expense of my devotion to him. This was something I had to learn while raising our sons. (I was not perfect, but I began to practice and allowed my sons to tell me when I handled this incorrectly.) My husband's dedication to the well-being of his family makes him look good because we represent him and what he is able to provide. When a man has a virtuous woman, it balances out all the good that God put in him. Although my husband and I are not always together, he is known everywhere that I frequent to and is spoken of very favorably.

> ***Proverbs 31:24–27: "She maketh fine linen, and selleth it; and delivereth girdles unto the merchant. ²⁵Strength and honour are her clothing; and she shall rejoice in time to come. ²⁶She openeth her mouth with wisdom; and in her tongue is the law of kindness. ²⁷She looketh well to the ways of her household, and eateth not the bread of idleness."***

In the twenty-first century, you hear all this talk about women entrepreneurs and the importance of several streams of income. This is not new. The virtuous woman is selling fine linen and delivering undergarments to be sold by the city's merchants. The woman is not lazy and is actually called strength. There are too many women making excuses for why they cannot do the things that would make their lives better. Where has this laziness come from? It may not be laziness, but it could have everything to do with physical and emotional self-care. They have done their bodies so poorly that they have little strength to even imagine creativity. But there are many who strive to conquer the world and just need to know how to do it correctly while pleasing a good man. You can be a millionaire wife and still be Mrs. Virtuous Woman.

I once read a Facebook post from a young lady that read, "Why do these good men overlook a well-educated, intelligent woman for a low-class woman that is aspiring to do nothing?" My first reaction was to wonder how he knew that she was so well educated and intelligent. Did she tell him that upon first meeting him? As mentioned early on in this chapter, no man wants to contend with arrogance when he knows nothing else about you. A virtuous woman is a woman of chaste character. Bragging has never been a desirable trait. The woman a man chooses may have more attributes that she does not flaunt, but allows to shine privately when the time is right.

Those men that must contend with a nagging woman who regularly flaunts her positives and constantly points out his flaws are doing their best to stay. Some leave or find contentment somewhere else. I would never justify a man hitting a woman, but I have heard some stories of the onset of some physical altercations that are very suspect. Besides the obvious attacks from spouses that need little to no provocation, some situations could have been avoided. A young lady came from a home where she watched her mother being constantly abused by boyfriends. She married a man from a two-parent home that saw no such treatment. Used to seeing the abuse, she would regularly get in his face attempting to make him hit her. One lady constantly berated her husband on the fact that he did not make as much as her. Another constantly talked about the fact that he lived in "her" house. Yet another young lady thought that she was better than her husband because he grew up in a single-parent home in the inner city while she was raised in middle-class suburbia with both parents. She also had attended an Ivy League college. How was this supporting her husband? What should have been his response to these underhanded insults? If you find yourself in any of these categories, both of you go to counseling before something happens that you will later regret. Some men have no answer to being antagonized. It is really not fair to say whatever you want, knowing that the man has no defense. Recall that the virtuous woman opens her mouth using wisdom. Some women must unlearn what they saw with their own eyes.

> **Proverbs 31:28: "Her children arise up, and call her blessed; her husband also, and he praises her."**

You want to live your best life, then do not nag or spend time with other women who do. Your speech should be tempered with wisdom and kindness. If you are a working woman, you do not have time for idle chatter. Your household is a priority as you keep an eye out for the future. For the record, nagging can be as simple as asking your spouse over and over to do the same thing. What kind of image are you making for your children? Even if a woman has no children, her image is seen by other young people. There is always someone watching. Children watch, and a husband is glad with a woman who wants the best for her family. These scriptural references are what happen spiritually when the woman follows the principles. You do not have to make the results take place; that is what God will do. Do the principle and watch the return.

A wise woman once told me that when she had problems with her husband, she would take it to God. I wondered how, and she explained that God made him and knew how to fix the inner workings of his heart. God would have greater success than she could with her mouth. I would like to tell you that what she told me does work. You just have to shut down your emotions, remember to pray and make some inner and physical changes to how you operate

A virtuous woman is at the top of the scale. When this woman makes it a priority to do all things godly, she will always be praised. She will benefit from all that she does and her reputation will precede her. I cannot imagine any woman that would not want this accolade.

> **Proverbs 31:30–31: "Favour is deceitful, and beauty is vain; but a woman that fears the Lord, she shall be praised. Give her the fruit of her hands; and let her own works praise her in the gates."**

This Proverbs 31 woman is a picture of the kind of woman that God designed. She is not just a help to a man, but an asset to all of creation. What would this world be without women? Proverbs 31 sums up the discourse by saying that looks will leave and all else is vain, but the woman that fears the Lord is worthy of praise. When you understand this fear to be honor and reverence, you will strive to live there. Who would not want to serve a God that promises such prosperity just for governing your life under his guided power? That is the answer for all that Proverbs 31 discusses. Respecting God's order for what it returns is reason enough to get back to the original design. You are a queen and should strive to act like one.

A young man once said that all the talk he heard as a child growing up in church made him shun the prospect of having a virtuous woman for a wife. There weren't many sermons that he could understand that explain the virtuous woman other than a prude that wore long skirts and any young man would have a hard time drawing her close. What is funny about that is found in the word virtuous itself. If you do an etymology on the word virtue, you will find that the prefix vir means man. Virtue's definition includes such accolades as moral excellence and chastity. A virtuous woman is far from a woman who is helpless and looking for rescue, or even a dowdy woman who dares any man to come near.

Remember that in the Garden, God called both the man and the woman Adam (Genesis 5:2). He created them equal in complimenting ability, but the elder or older was given authority. That is not a strange concept to any family. The man and the woman were working together. What interrupted that was their disobedience to one simple rule. Adam caused every human after that to be born into a sinful world. Jesus brought back the equality when he died on the cross. His crucifixion represented the punishment for all who sinned from Adam to the present. We are once again "one," working in unison to fulfill our individual and joint purpose.

All you single women, there is a place for you in this world. Whether married, single, or heading down the aisle, your place has been set in history. This world was made a better place when God made you. Single women can ascribe to doing the same things that all other virtuous women do. You can even do it better. You have time to work on yourself in the peace and quiet of your own place without the interruption of needs of a husband. Oh, you did not know that having a husband is sometimes an interruption. Just get one. You'll see when you are snoring and he taps you on your back for some attention after he had plenty of attention last night, or everyone is sitting down for dinner and he asked for some more water before you have taken your first bite. It can get to be fun after a while, if you make all this stuff part of the habits of marriage! The intrusion of children is a little easier because you can control their interference with your personal time. Use your time wisely, so that you will be an asset to yourself. Whether you ever get married or not, there will never be a question of how you represent the species. You have all the time you need to fulfill your God-given dreams. Make it happen!

Marriage is an institution set up by God. One of the largest problems that I have found is the lack of understanding that each sex has for the other. Mothers have long subscribed to telling their daughters how to be ladylike. That's great if all mothers actually knew what that meant. Ladies were built to be tough. I was tough and tried to hide that fact. I remember finding out how to add water to the battery in my car and not telling my husband for fear that I would be taking away his masculinity. That was crazy because I met him while we were both in the army. Then there was that time that I thought I had done something when I talked my then twelve-year-old son through changing my flat tire. Who can forget the time that my brake light was out and the dealership was going to charge me $75 to change it? I looked in the owner's manual of my Volkswagen and showed my nephew where to find the fuse that I had to replace: $12.50. Boy, you could not tell me anything. After my husband paid to have the floors tiled in the basement, my lady den was left out because at the time it had decent carpeting. Five years later, the carpet was ready to be changed. I went to a carpet remnant store and bought what I needed and laid my own carpet. At this point, knowing what I know now, I say, "So what" to that. No, there is nothing wrong with yielding the floor to a man, but a damsel in distress is a consequence of the pitiful woman who has been cursed and desires a man so much that she will do anything to get his attention. A man loves a woman that knows her way through life, but can also help manage his. So get married, but please maintain your independence. This *is* the way God set marriage up: The church as the bride of Christ is regularly preparing itself for its groom; the groom, Christ, among other things, is getting ready to come for his bride for her to live eternally in the place being prepared.

On earth, you represent the bride, the church, and the husband represents the groom, Christ; and this is the perfect picture of the great marriage of Christ and the church (Ephesians 5:22–33).

Those men out there that may be threatened by a strong woman, leave them alone. There are plenty of women that will remain the Cinderellas of the world. But you should not have to hide your virtuosity simply to help maintain his silly pride. Get you a man where the two of you can overtake your domain.

Training to be a full-fledged virtuous woman requires one set of rules and they are described in one word: planning. In that planning, there are many things to consider, but the top ones are time management, assertiveness, budgeting, and the biggest of all: creativity. If you are in that fifth of unmarried women that some surveys say are unapproachable, then you need to learn how to approach. That is one of those things that society says is up to the man. I have heard too many stories from women who say that a man will act interested, but then the next move never comes. You have nothing to lose by making the next move. Men get rejected regularly. Women over the years had some bad advice and have really messed up. The man is left to go after women, capture one, marry her, and then think that they are responsible for her entire life. It is time for that lie to end. If you ask my husband, he will tell you that I asked to marry him. My full-fledged virtuousness does not remember anything like that!

Chapter Six

Add It Up

This book is the result of answering a request. After a masterclass on the twenty-first-century virtuous woman, one of the two hundred attendees made the statement to me that there was so much content discussed that it needs to be in a book. She adds that the subject is content-heavy and that there is no way she or many others will be able to contain the information. So here it is. This is your class handout.

Okay, I started out with the story of Adam and Eve. Adam was created first and given the duty of naming all the animals while taking dominion over the earth. Eve was created as a helper to Adam. I do not know why being a helper became such an insult. What I know about God is that he loves balance and orderliness. How would it have been if both man and woman were both in charge? I find that my willingness to submit to authority makes me more powerful. But even with the order of Adam being first, the situation still became a mess. Eve disobeyed and then invited her husband to join her in her wrongdoing.

Every nation does not make women second-class citizens, but many do. This is a reality across racial and cultural lines. I find no other reason for this other than what happened in the Garden of Eden. The evidence of the disparity is apparent in many marriages and the identical thoughts about women expressed in many places.

This book was designed to bring about a difference in the thought process. One's perception is one's truth. If you want to drastically change any area of your life, then you must change your perception about how things are *supposed* to work in that area. How men and women interact has followed the picture of what happened after the punishment. Very few have even discussed the reentrance of what should have been after Christ became the second Adam. This is a do-over for all humans. God has superseded himself from punishment of his creation to all-encompassing redemption. Jesus freed all of mankind. There is no ugliness. The return to the original design is only made possible for you by understanding what Christ did on the cross: repentance, receiving forgiveness, and walking in the Kingdom that does not come from observation, but spiritual revelation (Luke 17:20).

The proof of redemption is found in the study of how God sent his son, Jesus. Jesus' life on earth, death, burial, and resurrection is a perfect picture of what God keeps presenting to his creation. There is a better way. I see nowhere that God said that saving people from sins is just for men. The Kingdom of God presented by Jesus is designed for all humans. When you live in the lane that is designed for you, there is prosperity that can be enjoyed by only you. I live with an alpha male and I know who he is in my life, but I also know who and what I am to him and the world. This Kingdom mindset is better than submitting to laws and the oppression of fighting something that has been given a clean slate by Jesus' death on the cross. Human spiritual freedom is not just so that all can get to eternal life; it also pertains to how you live on this earth.

Not only did women have a place in the Bible days, but God gave them some authority to direct great undertakings. There was Deborah in the book of Judges that stood as a judge for a period. Although childless, she was called the mother of Israel (Judges 5:7). You hear Apostle Paul telling his spiritual son, Timothy, to activate the gifts bestowed on him that was passed down from his grandmother and mother (2 Timothy 1:6). Did you think God did not consider women in setting up order?

The biggest battle to me has been women flaunting who they know they are and men usurping their authority in answer to this. None of this ever ends in peace. For that reason, I take my place in joy and thrive in the peace that God has already set up. I have no reason to fight. The battle is already won. God empowers purpose. The only way to end turmoil is a return to purpose. I found out that God can turn things around if you adjust and live in purpose. You will be walking in your gifts, and God will ensure that you stand before the great (Prov. 18:16).

The book of Esther is an example of the submitting powerful wife that knew how to accomplish what she was purposed to do. She did not hide her beauty, but she hid what would soon be an asset. In the 2011 movie *Jumping the Broom*, the bride's mother is a doting housewife living in a mansion only accessible by boat on Martha's Vineyard. The husband seems to be having an affair with his trusted assistant. The real reason for the husband and assistant's clandestine meetings was to discuss the status of his company. Toward the end of the movie, it is revealed that his company is failing and he is nearly bankrupt. His wife surprises him with a stash that she has kept from him. They are able to stay afloat with this treasure. Esther keeping her heritage a secret until the right time enables her to save her people and live out the rest of her days in harmony while being cherished by her admiring husband, the king. Fulfilling your purpose sometimes calls for you to hide certain assets until the time is right for them to be revealed!

I am not sure how many times I have heard some women talking about their great worth and the men that reject them because of it. Why is your great worth so important? Are you trying to buy a man? Even if your love interest or spouse adores that you are degreed and make a high six figures, he does not want you to wave this over his head. It's a profound confidence builder for you, but a great asset to his dreams. The flaunting of assets is what will get you in trouble. Making a man feel like you do not need him is a sure way to turn him off. There has to be more to you than how much money you have inherited or made on your own.

Surprising your man with your great worth is better than having him despise your supposed "assets." Many people are not jealous of you; they despise you. Jealous people wish they were you. Those that despise you are sick of hearing what you have. Be quiet. Some people are happy where they are, and what you have does nothing for them. A man is not different. If he wants something from you, he knows how to ask. You can yank it out at the right time and show your real worth, and both of you will win.

Now here is the real kicker. Proverbs 31 describes a woman that can rule the world, but she is content to make her husband and children look good with all her accolades. I love this. Remember that this scripture is what a wise king wrote from the properties that his mother told him to look for in a virtuous woman that would be his queen. The most powerful and gracious women I know are the ones who have a quiet intrigue. Now, that is something to strive for. The "ous" at the end of virtuous means full of, abounding in, possessing the qualities of. She can rule the world, but is happy helping her man do that with her by his side. Both are on top, the king and the queen together.

Do away with arrogance and all those things that make any person ugly. Keep striving to be the best at whatever it is that you do. Be that woman whose worth is greater than rubies. Can you imagine that you have a doctorate, live in a modest condo with your three children, and a strong man finds interest in you? You're not dumping the burden of paying all of your bills on him. What if you are a line worker in McDonald's but have been wise in your spending? You keep yourself up, love the Lord, and have discovered three other streams of income. You do not have an abundance to offer in the way of material assets, but you are virtuous and compare yourself in private to no one but the person you used to be. There is nothing wrong with either of these visions. Attitude is everything. You will be a perfect addition as long as you walk in your authenticity. (All that arrogance is not!)

Chapter Seven

No Clue

Talking about being authentic, not only did I have to learn about living my true self, I am getting ready to be really transparent with you. I wanted you to understand what I had to learn. It was not learned overnight. My true living as a full virtuous woman did not come until years of practice that started after I was forty-three. You have to be comfortable with your own history in order to embrace being authentic. I cannot change history, but use it as a platform for my now.

There is nothing that ever happened to you that is too ugly for God to consider in your trajectory to freedom. He knows all about you and allowed whatever you went through to get you to where you are today. Unless you are six feet under and cannot read this book, you are here for a reason. The most intriguing people I have ever come in contact with have been those that can sit erect and tell me things about themselves that sound almost impossible for any human to have endured. I love it. That is my blueprint for life.

All things really do work together to make you better (Romans 8:28). No, all things are not good, but God is in control of the universe. Nothing escapes his grasp. He created it all. Everything lines up to help you. I read the story of Joseph in the Bible many times. I see in it the story of a conceited scrawny teenager who thought he was greater than his entire family. Yes, God had promised him some great things, but they would not be manifested in an inexperienced teenager. Unfortunately, the prophecy was too much for little Joseph to contain. He shared his dreams with his entire family. He had to experience seventeen years of anguish because he did not know how to keep his mouth shut. Even in that, God used every bit of Joseph's days to get the glory out of his ability to dream and decode them, *and* to humble him in the process. By the end of Joseph's bondage as a servant in the military leader's house and a long stint in jail, Joseph said that interpretation of dreams belonged to God (story found in Genesis 37–50). What a change had come over him. This is the life that I am talking about when you acknowledge that all things work together for good.

Sixteen years ago, I wrote a little book called *The Curse of Jezebel*. I did not have it published, but shared it with friends and family members. My mother was so enamored with the book that she shared it with her pastor's wife, who instantly copied it and gave it to a group of ladies as a foundational text for a class.

The information was very personal. The book was a teaching about Jezebel, but it was also a testimony. I had not and still have not heard more than one person, other than me, admit that she/he operated in the spirit of Jezebel.

I had no clue why I had such a hard time submitting to authority. Military life, four years of college, and seventeen years as an influential church member did nothing to stem the tide of my rebellious thinking and tough exterior. The toughness had nothing to do with being virtuous. I submitted, but it was only in physical form; my inner being was crying out to escape.

My pastor in 1999, Rogers Murray, of Victory Family Life Church in Lithia Springs, saw my angst. He did all he could to help me, but God knew that it was an inside job. I had to want to be delivered. At that time, I did not know that I needed to be delivered. I had lived like this for over thirty-seven years. I can say that now, but did not know this in 1999.

I grew up in church and had a holiness-or-hell preacher for a father. He taught us the Word every Tuesday night from the confines of our couch. On occasion, the entire family would be on a fast (announced from a huge note taped to the refrigerator). When I think back, there is one scripture that I never really understood until now. I had always heard about the broad road leading to destruction and the narrow difficult road that leads to life (Matthew 7:13–14). I equated this to heaven and hell. It is not until this season that I understand Jesus to be talking about living in his Kingdom on earth versus living the best I can on my own. The difficulty in finding the stance in this mindset is faith. This Kingdom of God is inside and must come by way of revelation, not observation (Luke 17:20). I never understood this, even when coming from a dogmatic-believing father talking to his family on a Tuesday evening in the living room.

I get it now! Sin in the Garden of Eden separated us from our God in heaven, but Jesus came to reconcile God's creation back to him! The only connection is through Jesus' spirit that resides in all believers. The word says reconciled because creation was fully connected to God in the Garden and was disconnected by sin (Romans 5:10). By one man's sin, everyone is called a sinner and by one man's obedience, Jesus, everyone gets reconnected (Romans 5:19).

Getting born again did not stop my actions of rebelliousness. I knew that I could not be saved living like I wanted, so I forced myself as best I could to live right. According to scripture, laws can never save us. I guess that is why with every new scripture revelation, I thought I was just getting saved again. The Word could not penetrate deeply. I kept trudging along. Thirty-seven years being oppressed by rebellion and seventeen years since salvation (Oh wow, there is that number again!), God was going to pull me through.

It started with a guest preacher coming to my church on a Sunday evening in 1992. He preached a message about the spirit of Jezebel. It struck a chord in me. I knew so many people who attempted to control everything around them. Some women refused to submit to their husbands. They always had an excuse that centered on what their husbands were not. I paid attention to the men who controlled those around them with dominating personalities. You could see this in those strong single parents and those men that ruled with their personalities. It was never gentle and it normally stung like an iron fist. I wanted to help all of these people that this preacher was talking about that were bound by this spirit of manipulation and control. He said that it could be demonstrated in men or women. This preacher woke something up in me and I took on the position of the "deliverer."

The information never left my conscious mind, but I soon gave up my "witch hunt" because I had no clue how to get the people out of the situation. It would be seven years before I would hear about this again.

In 1998, I was struggling financially, but did not want to tell my husband how horribly off I was. The house was almost in foreclosure. We had only been in it for twelve years. I had already taken out the max of three loans from my 401(k). I was ignorant of a hardship withdrawal and decided to think of another way to get money out of it. I would have to leave my employment at the bank to get the entire balance after they recovered the loan balances. Yes, I could handle this burden all by myself (although my husband was not only gainfully employed and made nearly twice as much as I did).

It was during this time that my pastor's wife wanted to start her second day care since the other had closed nearly thirteen years prior. She knew I loved kids as evidenced by my regular work in the children's department and the fact that I started the children's church from scratch. She asked me if I would direct the undertaking. I thought about it for approximately two minutes and told her yes. Here was the answer to all my problems. I could leave my job, get my money, and then have an income from watching children. This offer could not have come at a better time.

One month after leaving my gainful employment as the trainer for all customer service representatives at a major bank, I found myself in the foyer of the church directing a summer camp (the infant stage of the new day care). There was no stove in this building, although we did have a basement. It would be a full week with the pastor's wife bringing breakfast at 7 a.m. and leaving to prepare lunch at about 11 a.m. that the pastor made a suggestion. Since there were only six children, maybe my husband would allow me to start the day care from home. The plan was set and on the following Monday beginning at 6:30 a.m., six two- to four-year-olds were dropped at my house.

When the school year started, there were five two- to four-year-olds and one infant at my house. Thank God for a basement and extra rooms for nap time. My day started at 5 a.m. I promised God that if he helped me every day to rise, shower, dress, and prep for breakfast and lunch, I would start preparing fresh breakfast and lunch for my husband during the week. That started and continues up to now. It was not until the following April that my church congregation moved into a larger facility with a commercial kitchen that the day care left my home.

Before the school year ended, flyers were put out at the local elementary schools advertising the upcoming summer camp season. By the first week of June, there were fifty children aged five to twelve registered for the camp.

For some reason before summer camp started, I felt compelled to ask for information about prayer from the two leaders of our church's intercessory prayer team. One gave me some verbal information, but the other had been to a conference with Morris Cerullo (a world-renowned evangelist and teacher) about prayer and deliverance. This particular leader lady gave me a green folder wrapped in cellophane paper that she had received while at the conference several years before this time. Preparing for the summer session was very time consuming; I put the package up for later reviewing.

The camp started off without a hitch, but toward the end of the camp, the children grew restless and ready for school. There was a shortage of assistants and the smaller children that were too young for the camp still had to be cared for. When two six-year-olds, as a joke, decided to dial 911, the camp ended early before prepping for the upcoming school year could begin. I was now unemployed. The camp went from smooth sailing to choppy waves.

Here I was in September, short of income after promising my husband, before leaving the bank, that he would never have to be concerned that my portion of the bills would be neglected. My promise now had to be broken. After thoroughly cleaning the house and cooking dinner, I decided that I now had time for some prayer and relaxation. As I stood before my fireplace in this empty house, I asked the Lord a question that would prove to be the beginning of a transformation in my life. "Lord, if you would, please do not let my husband be mad when I tell him that he must cover my portion of the bills!" I never expected to hear an audible answer. I actually just hoped that God would just make my request a reality, but I clearly heard. "You do not love that man; you just want to control him!" I was shocked and began to argue with God. (Thank God for mercy!) I answered that I recognized that as Jezebel and that could not be me. I heard nothing else and felt no comfort that God would allow my husband to be content with my request.

I decided to lie on top of my clean covers on the bed and open the package on prayer that I had not had a chance to look at before. I propped the pillows and sat down on the bed. I began to unwrap the cellophane from around the folder. When the folder was opened, I could see in the right pocket a decorated professional pamphlet from the prayer conference and on the left was several sheets of white print paper folded down and stapled at the top. I unfolded the papers and was slapped right in the heart. Typed across the top of the front page in bold letters were the words "Deliverance from the Curse of Jezebel!" This could not be happening. There was no denying what I had just heard after prayer, and now here on my bed would be the beginning of *my* deliverance.

Not sure what was going to happen after this encounter. I read through the typed papers and the description could have been adopted from spending a month in my life. There was no way around this; I had been living oppressed by an evil force of a Jezebel. I did not know that it was oppression until after months of praying and studying the story of Jezebel in the Bible (starting at 1 Kings 16:29). I had known before now that the Holy Spirit will not live in someone possessed by a devil. How could I be saved yet operate in evil? I was comforted by the fact that there was a difference between oppression and possession. When possessed, you have no control of your spirit. The enemy lives at will and has the ability to direct thoughts and actions. Oppression can mimic the same, but the Holy Spirit is more powerful and constantly warns the believer that there is something askew. I evidently had not heard the previous two warnings: first when the preacher had come seven years prior and one more time when my pastor talked about submitting to God, so that submitting to authority would not be such a strain. I knew now that God really loved me. I was now becoming aware of what was going to happen to me. God had set me up, so that one person planted the truth, my pastor watered the truth, and now God was growing the truth in me (1 Cor. 3:8).

As I studied, I wrote and this was the inception of the first little book. Some months past and the subject matter surfaced periodically. The first manuscript was lost and the computer was eventually given away. It was the second writing that I printed and sent to my mother and gave a few copies to some local friends. That was the end of that. I still see Jezebel operating in those who have no clue. It manifests in manipulation and control over people, in the inability to apologize and talking over people in constant defense. My witch hunt did not take place this time. When I began to write the first manuscript, I asked a friend about why no one would admit or confess like I had. She told me that once you are truly delivered, judging others outside of love is the furthest thing from your mind. I knew then that there was a lot more work for me from the inside. I understood clearly now about one person planting a seed, another person watering, and God giving the increase (1 Cor. 3:8). How easy it is to forget, and it took all three of these instances to turn my life around. There is a sincere desire that all would cross paths with someone who would give them a word that may stir a change. The study still continues.

The unction to rewrite the book just surfaced. It will actually be the third writing. The first one was rank with few facts and some misinformation. I did not know enough to talk about the subject. I became frustrated and never shared the contents. That was 1999. 2001 is when the second edition came into being.

Here it is, 2020 and the third writing. The actions of many have not changed and now there is an entire generation of people who matured into young adulthood who can benefit from knowledge of this information. Prayerfully, I can plant or water many more. Whether the person publicly confesses or not is inconsequential. Getting free is paramount.

I am sincerely praying that many who read this and struggle in this area would be open to accept the truths about themselves. Living in bondage is not obvious when you are not made aware. I just thought there was a dysfunction in my upbringing that made me have the hard character flaw. Apologies were hard coming, but if I wanted to sleep well, they had to be given. Now, they can flow off of my tongue with little to no fanfare. I still pray for me and others, because the enemy knows your weakness and that will be his area of constant attack. My greatest defense is power intrinsic in my salvation and my personal testimony that I will share with you shortly.

The woman at the well encountered Jesus, who told her about her entire life. She may have wanted to reject the fact that she needed the water that Jesus offered her, but his direct line into her life left her with no way of escaping the truth. She was thirsty and needed the water that would make her never thirst again (story found in John 4). Jesus was God in the flesh and could see straight through her like He did me. This is the hope of the writing in this chapter, that you will see yourself (if you struggle here) and want a change.

Believe it or not, this concept is not as blatant and only shows up in demonstrative women, as you may think. The most docile of personalities may sometimes incorporate manipulation and control. Although Jezebel, in the Bible, brought prostitution in the temple and tempted men with a bandanna on her head and painting her face that is far from her only wrongs (story in 1 Kings 16 and 2 Kings 9). Jezebel's main task was to silence the voice of the prophet. In everyday terminology, Jezebellic ways are those that are unable to submit. Abhorring authority is a mainstay. Although someone who deals with manipulation and control may not blatantly disobey, he/she may find a way to manipulate or control his way out of a directive. Many biblical scholars have studied the name Jezebel to come to a comprehensible etymology. The one that matches how I lived is "without cohabitation."

Chapter Eight

Preacher on a Sunday Night

It was a Sunday night in the summer of 1992 and there was a guest speaker in our sanctuary. About fifteen minutes into the message, my curiosity piqued. "Jezebel is not just a lady of the evening. She uses manipulation and control to get what she wants," came from the preacher's mouth. What? I have heard women called Jezebel for wearing too much makeup or dressing provocatively, especially if they had a red dress on. Now, the preacher is saying that Jezebel manipulated people in order to control them and that this spirit can be used by a "she" or "he."

I was thoroughly enlightened by this new information and could not wait to test the waters. I was familiar with quite a lot of people who I could place in this category. Some would always take authority in every conversation. They could never be wrong, or, under any circumstance, apologize. Even if the apology would ease someone's pain, it was not going to happen.

I analyzed what the preacher said and figured a way to present the information to those that needed to be "delivered." "Have you ever considered that maybe your strong personality is a result of a somewhat controlling way of conducting your life?" was my approach. My listeners would ponder the question and justify why their seemingly controlling ways were being misunderstood. I asked it of men and women with the same outcome.

My research continued. I watched women that spoke for their husbands. Observing wives who criticized their spouses in public became a pastime. Then there were the women that made all the decisions in the household to their husbands' displeasure. There were plenty of other instances, but a man who nagged was a distant last. I guess that is because my research would not let me see what is rarely discussed.

In all my analyzing and sharing, no one could see themselves. After several months and no continued talk from anyone else, I gave up my saving ways. There were no takers on this go round. After all, it was a demon that I was attempting to get believers to say was using them. Oh well, maybe in the future.

Chapter Nine

Who Is This Jezebel Anyway?

As stated earlier, I grew up with a preacher for a father. Hearing about the lake of fire and God's wrath was a regular occurrence in my house. At the age of six, I almost drowned when I jumped into a pool that was ten feet deep at its furthest end. I immediately developed a fear of water. I would not allow the shower water to splash into my face and washing my hair was a horrendous affair. One night, I dreamt that I fell into a bathtub and it had no bottom. I awoke petrified. My dad told me that it was the bottomless pit that is talked about in the book of Revelation. So now I am afraid of water *and* going to hell. The real point of the paragraph is to tell you that I heard about Jezebel on the regular. My dad talked about her in the house to his six daughters and one son and regularly referenced her from the pulpit at church gatherings. Anything that resembled evil, we were taught about it.

All I knew about Jezebel was that she was a lady of the evening; that was until the guest preacher came and talked about her right from the story in the Bible. I enjoyed the teaching, but did not get enough in that one night. I went home and began to study.

1 Kings 16 tells of King Ahab marrying Jezebel, who did not worship God. Not only was she an unbeliever, but she was allowed to bring her worship of Baal (a false god) into the temple of the true God. The worship of Baal and Asherah involved sexual promiscuity. Jezebel, as the state

sponsor of the promiscuity, was the Prostitute of Babylon (http://www.biblenews1.com/babylon/babylon4.html#Prostitute).

Jezebel had all the prophets of God that she could gather slaughtered. Obadiah, because of his high regard for the one true God, hid one hundred believers in two caves, shielding them from Jezebel's wrath (1 Kings 18:4).

One act loomed large in the scripture, proving how actually ruthless and ungodly Jezebel was. But before discussing this act, let us look at what enabled Jezebel to operate like this in the land of Israel. "And Ahab the son of Omri did evil in the sight of the Lord above all that were before him" (1 Kings 16:30). After all, we must recall that it was King Ahab who married Jezebel in the first place. Jezebel's reigning terror was a result of what her husband allowed. The manipulation and control of the enemy by way of Jezebel made its ultimate appearance when Jezebel decides to carry out the desires of her husband by conniving circumstances.

It is so unnerving that God created the virtuous woman to be so powerful, but power in the unregenerate soul can wreak havoc. It is so very easy to think that your role as helper could become manipulative. You know what is best and the person will have to yield to the control. This is not God's way, though. He would never require a human to use evil tactics to get another human to submit to him. That is why dominion for humans is over the earth and all its inhabitants other than other humans. Being virtuous is a godly thing, not sensual.

God had a plan to stop evil now, just like he did when Jezebel was doing her best dirt. Nothing catches God off guard. My activities and the actions of others are God's opportunities for intervention. Back then, God sent his prophet, Elijah, to bring a change to a country that denounced God and worshipped idols. Elijah's first prediction was a drought that would last until he said it was over. The drought lasted three years (1 Kings 18:1).

You would think that after suffering a devastating three-year drought that some soul-searching would take place, but that is just the way this manipulation and control thing works. I suffered for thirty-seven years, seventeen of those years while contending with the Holy Spirit working on drawing me closer to God. This spirit will never admit defeat and of course never be wrong. It would be 1 Kings 21 before you see one of the most horrendous displays of this spiritual war. The act would be the epitome of manipulation and control.

King Ahab found a plot of land near his palace that he thought would be a good place to plant a vegetable garden. The owner of the land, Naboth, had inherited the land from his father and according to law could not accept King Ahab's offer of a better property or money for this one. King Ahab went away depressed about Naboth's answer.

At the palace, King Ahab lay in bed depressed and refused to eat. Jezebel asked about his countenance. When she hears the reason, she tells him to get up and eat and that she would get the land for him. She forges the King's signature on a letter to the nobles of the domain where Naboth lived, saying that Naboth had cursed the King and God. She had Naboth brought down to a trial and found guilty by way of two witnesses that lied about Naboth's character. He was put to death. King Ahab's depression was now quieted. The day I opened that folder, I read something similar. Some unwitting good men benefit from this spirit's antics. I think about my finagling of budgets to convince my husband of my "superior" knowledge of budgeting. This was nothing but mess and it only led to misery. My palace was being pulled down by my own hands (Prov. 14:1)

It happened when King Ahab went to claim "his" property that he encountered Elijah. Elijah, following the Word of God, told King Ahab that God would destroy him and his family. Ahab, after hearing this pronouncement, humbled himself and fasted in repentance. God had mercy on him and told Elijah to tell him that he would not bring this calamity on this generation, but on the generation of his son. In 2 Kings 9 comes the end of Jezebel and her sons. Elisha (Elijah's successor) is instructed to anoint Jehu as king. After Jehu becomes king, he immediately kills Jezebel's sons. Soon after their deaths, he encounters Jezebel in a window. She pins up her hair and puts on face paint. As she taunts Jehu, he asks who is on his side. Jezebel's eunuchs are encouraged to throw her out of the window. This they do. Jehu has by this time confirmed that these deaths will avenge the senseless killing of Naboth and all of the evil brought to Israel by King Ahab and his wife, Jezebel. There is nothing left to bury of Jezebel's body. Her blood is splattered and dogs destroyed her corpse. So much for Jezebel's trickery of owning more properties. The virtuous woman knows how to save and find her own property. A woman operating as she should can curtail the selfish, immature ways of her man by just being virtuous.

As you continue to read this chapter, you must understand that although Jezebel is a human being, she is being used by Satan himself. Manipulation and control in these instances are strictly evil forces. You can see why no born-again believer would want to believe that he/she could be influenced by such a force, especially from evil. However, you must understand as I explained before that there is a difference between possession and oppression. Believers who walk in the Holy Spirit can only be oppressed. This is the case with all believers who struggle in a particular area and can find no place for deliverance. Oppression is evidenced by evil influence or suppression on the person's thoughts to make right decisions (http://www.differencebetween.net/miscellaneous/religion-miscellaneous/difference-between-oppression-and-possession/). The enemy's only job is to thwart the purpose of God in the life of a believer.

As a believer, you must understand that your body is the temple of the Holy Ghost, so demonic possession is impossible (1 Cor. 6:19). All the enemy can attempt to do is press upon the believer to act indifferent to the will of God in her life. You can see the contrast of being virtuous and attempting to act on your own apart from what God has already prepared for you to walk into. I can tell you all of this because, as you are made aware, I was such a believer!

Chapter Ten

Being Virtuous Will Happen

You would think that after all of this research and knowing about an ugly thing that I would make sure that something like that was far from me. That is just not how the enemy works.

As I began to write about my encounter and what I was learning through study, a thought dashed my peace. How could this alpha man that married me have dealt with my foolishness all these years? I learned a valuable lesson about the status of the human mind along with how men operate. When I asked God how my husband had lived with something so unvirtuous and so cunning, the answer came quickly as I crossed the threshold from one room to the next: "Man is no match for a demon!" Neither my husband nor most that knew me well had any idea of what troubled me. It could only have been revealed by God to someone who would handle me correctly. God had no intention of hurting me. He made my deliverance as gentle as only God could. He knew that teaching about the virtuous woman was in my future. What are you fighting with that may be blocking your purpose? Not only could my husband not know, except it be revealed by God, my ministry to him did not stop. Although I had messed up the finances on many occasions, my goal was always to do what the virtuous woman would do. God had been behind the scenes working the entire time to bring peace to a hurting soul.

This is quite an oxymoron—as unvirtuous as I was, I wanted to deliver all those other folks even before I overcame. It must have been what I call the mirror of other people. I could clearly see the problems in other's lives because they resembled the ones in mine. I was looking through evil-tainted glasses. Everyone is troubled but me. The answer was for me to take the long stick out of my own eye and then help those that asked (Matt. 7:5). It was totally hypocritical, pointing a finger out at others with three pointing back at me. As you see, the description of the virtuous woman was given to a king by his mother as he looked for the queen to rule with him. Get rid of the oxymoron, do not be as I was; put your crown on and *then* straighten your sister's crown.

The Lord allowed me to trace my life back, finding the root of Jezebel. I went back to the time when as a six-year-old girl, I was hospitalized with a bone infection. In December of 1961, emergency surgery was performed on my right thigh and I remained in the hospital for eight months. My mother was eight months pregnant and due in January. She also had two other children at home—my eldest sister, who is eighteen months older than me, and, at the time, my youngest sibling, who's twenty-one months younger than me. It was at this time that doctors would study the cause of my malady and watch the progress of healing through an open window on a body cast that held me still for many months.

One day, an orderly came to my hospital room and rolled me on a gurney to the basement level of the hospital. He parked the gurney on the side of the hallway and told me that in a moment, a doctor would come through the doors in front of me to bring me into that room. While waiting, a side door opened and an orderly in green scrubs splattered with blood came out. He looked over at me and asked if I would let him operate on me next. With no tremble in my voice and no fear that I can recall, I answered, "No!" It was then that I accepted that I was in control of my life and that I would never let anyone or anything intimidate me.

After this episode, the doors in front of me opened and a doctor came out to wheel me into this great room. My gurney was parked in the middle of this stage and to my right was a large screen with a camera showing the inside of my right leg and to my left was an elevated audience appearing as a sea of white coats. I laid there silent as no one was talking to me, but they were obviously discussing the plight of this little black girl with the afflicted right femur. To my young mind, the sea of white coats in this great room represented me against the rest of the world.

This was the day that I accepted Jezebel as the guide of my life. If I wanted preeminence on this earth, I would have to take it. Other than that, I was relegated to the sickly child who would soon die—keep her comfortable and do not consider her for a future. At six years old, I made the decision that this would not happen. Of course, I was not made aware of this until thirty-seven years later when I asked God when this evilness had begun to oppress me.

There is one part of this story that is somewhat blurry. I knew that I had been sick all of my life and my father would often pour oil on me and pray for me. But there was a particular time that my father was preaching at a strange church. My younger sister and I were in the back rows. During the altar call, my father beckoned for me to come up for prayer and I refused. In my subconscious, I believe that this happened before my long hospital stay. This would explain my encounter with Jezebel instead of the Holy Spirit. God gives a way of escape from all temptation (1 Cor. 10:13). God would not have it any other way. Although blurry, my heart seems to feel that what I believe about the timing of this occurrence is what actually happened.

As I continued to study my life with Jezebel, I came to realize that the sea of doctors came to represent all people. No one cared about me, but just wanted to gaze at my flaws. To have carried this burden in my mind all that time was pretty amazing for a person who still kept dreaming. Prayers were going up for me continually. I just had to battle with rejection. The Jezebel spirit did not care about me, but oppressed me for as long as I stayed ignorant.

This is a representation of what happens to most people. Gravitating to the oppression of what happens as a child lingers on to the future and blocks a full grasp of the will of God. Oppression stops clear thinking, doing the right thing with no dynamic thought of what God really wants. The result is partial victory. God always draws with love, but never forces his will on anyone. That is why believers are admonished to walk in the Spirit (of God). No purposeful walking will result in choices intercepted by the enemy. You may think that you chose right, but actually could have chosen what the enemy interjected. Minds not renewed to the ways of God are minds that lead people to wavering in decision-making.

Becoming a virtuous woman takes great purpose of thought. What you think must line up with God's way of thinking. Not submitting your thoughts to God's way results in choosing based on old personal experiences. Most of those old experiences come from the dysfunction that webbed its way into your life like all people as a result of living in a sinful world. Once knowing the greatness that is intrinsic in what God created for you propels you to choose the way God designed—virtuousness.

It would take some training not to revert back to my evil ways. As I encountered women with this same spirit, I was now equipped with a testimony. A fellow parishioner explained to me that when you have been through something, you have a lot more compassion than someone that knows something in theory. That makes sense. It sounds like what Jesus was talking about in Matthew 7. In this chapter, it does not tell believers not to judge; it says not to judge things that you know nothing about. Get delivered first, then you can see clearly how to help someone else. This is the way to stay away from evil ways, because now you are a living example of what not to do. When the next person wants what you have, they will run toward it. The other training was not to force your freedom onto someone else; give it to those that ask.

One night as I lay in bed reading, my husband told me that it was getting late and time to cut off the light. I kept reading for an additional ten minutes while at the same time ignoring his request. It struck me like a bolt of lightning. This is exactly one of the ways that I got my way. I just rebelled. When the truth hit me upside the head, I jumped up and immediately turned off the light. God knows how to spank you spiritually. If my husband would have gotten angry, I would have thought him wrong!

I finagled the budget without my husband's knowledge to purchase a car that we really could not afford. It was eventually repossessed. If the kids wanted to do something that I kind of knew my husband would not approve of without asking, I would approve. By the time he found out, it was too late. I never thought of my finagling as manipulation. Wrong number one: the kids should not have taken priority over my husband, and wrong number two: letting my pride lead when my pocketbook could not answer the call.

It was not until God spoke the word to me about controlling my husband that I knew that that is what I had been doing. I always thought of controlling as badgering, manhandling, or strong-arming. I never thought about my gentle conniving as controlling, but now, I was convinced of its reality in my life.

It is now twenty-one years later and I am studying about being virtuous. My husband and I are now empty nesters and things are totally different. I have taught a class in church about the virtuous woman of Proverbs 31 and have constantly strived to continue to live up to its tenets. God has done amazing things for me in the years that have passed. Change is possible. It does not have to take *you* thirty-seven years.

Although this chapter talks about this evil oppressing thing, it can oppress men. Either way, it is a disrupter of godly flow. How it uses men in other ways is important, but since this book is about women saving the male, content for another time makes sense.

Chapter Eleven

Here is How You Win

God is awesome. In the beginning, he designed a perfect existence. Proving that man could not operate outside of his power, Adam and Eve fell very quickly by disconnecting. In one of the Superman movies, Lois Lane gets to fly along with Superman as long as she stays connected to him. As the flight becomes more and more enjoyable, you watch as she starts out hooking her arm completely under his and then soon loosens her grip and slides her hand down to his. As they soar high above the clouds, she is now barely touching his hand. You see her eyes light up with excitement and she allows her hand to totally disconnect from the power source. Immediately, her flight takes a turn for the worst and she is quickly careening toward the ground. Superman must take a break from his glide to swoop down and fly up under Lois Lane before she is splattered on the ground below. God *is* awesome; he'll let you fly, but only if you stay connected to the power source.

Chapter Twelve

Started in Fear and Wins in Power

Manipulation and control is rooted in fear. Fear and faith are at different ends of the spectrum. "How do I succeed with all this negativity around me?" is what you ask. Your life may have had some dips that have consequences that will not go away. God is not hindered by any situation. He specializes in the worst-case scenarios. He always leaves a spot open where he can come in. He punished Eve and left a place in her lineage to plant his Son that would eventually save the world. God allowed a story like that of Esther to be put almost in the middle of the Bible. In that story is the secret to how God would redeem a world that was doomed to death. He is God and swears by himself because there is no one greater than him (Heb. 6:3). He will not change, but he can supersede himself. He said that all humans would die from sin and then he allows his Son to represent all men and die for everyone. No, man is not supposed to manipulate or control anything, but God can. He invented the concepts and can use them anyway he sees fit that will benefit all mankind and fulfill his purpose.

How much more power do people need when God said to have dominion over the earth? Every disruption comes from man thinking that God cheated some kind of way after the enemy introduced this concept onto the earth. Unfortunately, man took the idea and ran with it. The only way out of this dilemma is always available in God. The reason why God said not to fear is because he knows that with him, there is no fear. The authority to have dominion comes from the connection to God and this alone.

Once in my life, I came to realize that I was angry at God for many of my failings. I wanted to be a genius or at least highly intellectual, yet I have the least of that out of six children. Why was I the only sickly child? Oh, I could name several "complaints." It came to me that I wanted to forgive God. Wait! Don't get scared! God takes all complaints, depression, misinformation, etc. He loves you enough to hear all kinds of questions. Stop acting and tell yourself the truth. You may be hurting and have found no relief in how you are living or who you have lived with. God took my "foolish" thoughts and directed me to my purpose. Everything that I have and do not have is because purpose is more important. Just like Eve, I was more concerned about what was missing than what was already in my hand. My weakness is totally God's opportunity for his power (2 Cor. 12:9).

Never be afraid to ask or take your concerns to God. Sometimes, it will be as simple as forgiving yourself for being human. To be human is to error. Romans 7:20 says it the way many do not want to admit it—sin has control as long as it is allowed. There is always a way back to God. So you have not been virtuous and have messed up so much because of this. God knew this was going to happen. Number one, forgive yourself just like you know how to forgive others. Then take all that baggage and turn them into testimonies. Leave nothing out. Everything you have gone through was not to kill you; it was part of your purpose load. You must carry it with you and decorate it nicely. Every single thing is working out for your good if you love God and are being called into purpose (you are!) (Rom. 8:28). You see, no one threw me out of the window so that dogs could eat my body. Not only could I live after denouncing Jezebel, I came to a crossroad of what I called a "forgiving God." God showed me that I was mad because I did not understand. Don't be afraid, because God knows how to turn all lemons into lemonade.

The virtuous woman and the man dependent on her help is an awesome creation. You must understand that God operates in eternity where there is no time. Everything that ever will be is already created. God created man and then called him they. The woman was already created in spirit. He told Jeremiah that he knew him before he was seeded in his mother's womb by his father (Jer. 1:5). When the three Hebrew boys went into the fiery furnace, the king who had them put there saw Jesus, in physical form, walking in the fiery furnace way before he ever walked this earth and way before his mother was even born. God knew this day was coming when man would reteach how man and woman could get back to Eden before going into eternity to live with him forever. If you are reading this, there is time to redress in your virtuous garments.

When Jesus turned thirty, he started his ministry. He preached about a Kingdom that would not take place until after he died and rose and sent the Holy Spirit as a comforter and empowerment to mankind. While Jesus was teaching about the Kingdom of God, it was at the end of the time period called Law. The Kingdom of God that mankind is allowed to live in while living on earth is practice for the next time period called Kingdom. This last time period will be run by God in eternity, where no interruptions can possibly happen. Satan will be powerless and in hell. This is not a lesson in bondage, but complete freedom. It can only be perceived and lived in in a spiritually renewed mind. Why should you let Jesus' ministry be in vain and only benefit from his death on the cross that reoffers eternal life? There is so much more to live than being defeated while waiting to enter eternal life. Your attachment to God allows you to live in the expectation of eternal life while practicing for the perfection while still on earth. Jesus' Sermon on the Mount, preached during his ministry on earth, tells you how to get and stay in this spiritual Kingdom of God while still on earth (Matt. 5–7). You will not need this Kingdom of God when you are in the Spiritual Kingdom in eternity that has absolutely no evil infiltration.

Since God is in eternity and mankind is allowed to operate in time, everything that God created is available to man at all times. The status of the Garden and Eden is still open to receive. The cherubim yielding fire to keep man from the path to the tree of life is now gone for those that believe. God is the only one that can give life. As soon as Jesus died on the cross, the veil of the temple that separated man from entering the place where God's holiness rested was torn in two. This was God superseding his previous blockage to the tree of life. The partition is down. You can now get back to flying. All you have to do to reaccess what God has is to reconnect to the power source—God himself.

Man is destroyed for the lack of knowledge (Hos. 4:6). You want to say that you have not known some things but still have not been killed.

Compare this with Adam and Eve not dropping dead after they ate from the forbidden tree. But they did die and did not live forever on this earth as was planned. Your purpose is diminishing every day that you do not apply new knowledge that God allows you to hear. Your job as a believer is to apply new knowledge, then share it with others. You are empowered with the same authority that Jesus had when he came to earth—the ministry of reconciliation (2 Cor. 5:18).

The woman was taken out of man, and then every man born after Eve was created was taken out of a woman (1 Cor. 11:12). God has made everything equal and balanced. For a woman to help a man, she must be virtuous, which has some manliness about it. That is not strange. God called them both Adam. Just ask all those folks that have assisted big bosses for years. They remain in place because they had to become a little like the boss in order to assist him/her. Everyone is a spiritual being living in a natural body. In the spiritual realm, there is neither male nor female because everyone is one in Christ (Gal. 3:28).

Get in your purpose and prosper. You cannot lose doing it in God's way. One last plug, the practice in being a virtuous woman now in the Kingdom of God is not hard work like basic training in the army. You are already built for this walk. The hardest work will be in a change of mind. Everyone was born with a dysfunction. That does not hinder God's work. All that is needed is a decision to step right into your purpose and prospering by knowing that is all God ever wants from you.

Where are you today? Only you and God know, really. You may have been in and out of relationships, have four baby daddies, or are headed to your third marriage. Right now, this is all past tense. How will you spend the rest of your life? Can you see all those failings become testimonies? Rape, molestation, cancer, abuse, abandonment, homelessness, high school dropout, drug addiction, or any other thing like these cannot separate you from the love of God (Rom. 8:39). Where are you today? You are right in the place where you can hear from God.

I leave you with this entire chapter from Isaiah 54:1–17 (NIV). I tried to pull out one verse, but its refreshing Word continued to draw me farther down. Let the water of the Word wash you from any downfall you have ever experienced. The picture in this biblical chapter is the symbolism of a woman left feeling cheated because of what life has offered her for years. It is a reminder that God is in control and has reserved for you his best:

1 "Sing, barren woman, you who never bore a child; burst into song, shout for joy, you who were never in labor; because more are the children of the desolate woman than of her who has a husband," says the Lord.
2 "Enlarge the place of your tent, stretch your tent curtains wide, do not hold back; lengthen your cords, strengthen your stakes.
3 For you will spread out to the right and to the left; your descendants will dispossess nations and settle in their desolate cities.
4 "Do not be afraid; you will not be put to shame. Do not fear disgrace; you will not be humiliated. You will forget the shame of your youth and remember no more the reproach of your widowhood.
5 For your Maker is your husband—the Lord Almighty is his name—the Holy One of Israel is your Redeemer; he is called the God of all the earth.
6 The Lord will call you back as if you were a wife deserted and distressed in spirit—a wife who married young, only to be rejected," says your God.
7 "For a brief moment I abandoned you, but with deep compassion I will bring you back.
8 In a surge of anger I hid my face from you for a moment, but with everlasting kindness I will have compassion on you," says the Lord your Redeemer.
9 "To me this is like the days of Noah, when I swore that the waters of Noah would never again cover the earth. So now I have sworn not to be angry with you, never to rebuke you again.
10 Though the mountains be shaken and the hills be removed, yet my unfailing love for you will not be shaken nor my covenant of peace be removed," says the Lord, who has compassion on you.
11 "Afflicted city, lashed by storms and not comforted, I will rebuild you with stones of turquoise, your foundations with lapis lazuli.
12 I will make your battlements of rubies, your gates of sparkling jewels, and all your walls of precious stones.
13 All your children will be taught by the Lord, and great will be their peace.

14 In righteousness you will be established: Tyranny will be far from you; you will have nothing to fear. Terror will be far removed; it will not come near you.
15 If anyone does attack you, it will not be my doing; whoever attacks you will surrender to you.
16 "See, it is I who created the blacksmith who fans the coals into flame and forges a weapon fit for its work. And it is I who have created the destroyer to wreak havoc;
17 no weapon forged against you will prevail, and you will refute every tongue that accuses you. This is the heritage of the servants of the Lord, and this is their vindication from me," declares the Lord.

Afterthought

Hype to me is compared to fake. If something is too good to be true, it must be hype. I would dare not sell you hype. What I love about the Word of God is that it will never fail. It is such a good thing that you can always refer back to it. That is why God allows everything that is supposed to last to be written. Whether you forget or neglect to follow instructions, they are always available when you are ready to adjust. There is no hype in this book.

Staying in the will of God is a constant job of the believer. That is why the Word tells all to walk in the Spirit. As big as life is, it is only lived one step at a time. Each person's life is made up of millions of steps. Thank God for that, because one wrong step could have caused permanent damage to God's plan. Thank God for his mercy that this is not true. Because the Word also says in Proverbs 24:16 that the righteous fall seven times but gets up, but the wicked stumbles as soon as calamity strikes. The heart's desire to stay in the will of God is what protects the believer even when life hits hard. The wicked person will be utterly devastated because they have chosen evil.

Now that you understand the purpose of the virtuous woman, it will be your responsibility to regularly study her ways. Although you may fall off sometimes by mistake, you can rise again, steady yourself, and be ready for the next step.

Stay connected to the power source, my friends, so that you can always be correctly guided. Be blessed!

Lightning Source UK Ltd.
Milton Keynes UK
UKHW011011210820
368606UK00001B/162